Shalom Bayis

with a Twist of Humor

About the Author

JOE BOBKER was born in 1947 in Ulm, a displaced persons' camp in Germany, to Polish Holocaust survivors Chaskel, *zt"l*, and Ida Bobker. On May 21, 1949, the family arrived in Sydney, Australia, on board the *Luciano Marnaro* liner as refugees from Adolf Hitler's reign of terror. The most searing influences on his Jewishness were his parents, two simple Yidden who saw over a hundred family members turned into ashes by the genocidal Nazi war machine, yet never swayed from their beliefs. Their faith was clearer than vision.

Bobker studied at the renowned Mercaz HaRav Kook Yeshiva in Kiryat Moshe, Jerusalem. Over the years he has been a popular speaker and became well known for dozens of articles concerning Jews and Judaism in the one hundred-year-old *Los Angeles Jewish Times*, where he was publisher and editor in chief.

A prolific and creative writer, his books cover a variety of Jewish subjects emerging from an intimate yet philosophical, erudite and witty perspective.

Since 1980, Bobker has lived in both Los Angeles and New York with his wife Miriam, a barrister from Melbourne, Australia, also the child of Polish Holocaust survivors.

When asked where he gets his inspiration, Joe replied, "Eli, Avi, Benny, Dovi, Hadassa, Baylie, Layella, Devorah, Dalia, Toby, Chesky, Yoni, Boruch, Zevi, Mattie, Mordechai, Henny, Dovid, Shira, Asher, Gali, Daniel, Leah, Rivka, and Shoshana – my four sons, four daughters-in-law, granddaughters and grandsons (as of Pessach 2009)."

Other Books by the Author

Torah with a Twist of Humor

And You Thought There Were Only Four!
400 Questions to Make Your Seder More Enlightening, Educational and Enjoyable!

From Fasting to Feasting: A Unique Journey through the Jewish Holidays

Torah News U Can Use: I Didn't Know That!

Pirkei Avos with a Twist of Humor

Can I Play Chess on Shabbas?

Jewish Wisdom with a Twist of Humor

Shalom Bayis
with a Twist of Humor

7 Tips to a Healthy Marriage

JOE BOBKER

gefen
publishing house   בית הוצאה לאור גפן
JERUSALEM ♦ NEW YORK

Cover design and typesetting: S. Kim Glassman
Cover Art: Avi Katz

ISBN: 978-965-229-455-5
Edition 1 3 5 7 9 8 6 4 2

Gefen Publishing House Ltd.
6 Hatzvi St.
Jerusalem 94386, Israel
972-2-538-0247
orders@gefenpublishing.com

Gefen Books
600 Broadway
Lynbrook, NY 11563, USA
1-516-593-1234
orders@gefenpublishing.com

www.gefenpublishing.com

Printed in Israel

Send for our free catalogue

Contents

Acknowledgments

I would like to thank my mentor and teacher, HaRav Osher Abramson, *zt"l*, a Holocaust survivor, and my wife Miriam, who brings *shalom* into any *bayis*, wherever she goes. She can be found in the dictionary under patience, understanding, serenity, peace. Without her support this book – like all those that have preceded it – would still be lost in my drawer instead of displayed on your shelf!

Caveat

This book is not a halachic guide, nor a source of halachic domestic rulings. Its *sole purpose* is to open the curtain slightly on the subject of marriage and *middos* ("manners"), and encourage the reader to keep the premier mitzva of harmony in the home. The footnotes may not be entirely accurate, but will put the reader on the right path for further study and inspiration. If you have specific questions, ask a qualified rabbi.

Foreword

In his introduction to *Mesilas Yesharim*, Moshe Chaim Luzzato writes:

> I did not write this essay to teach people things they don't
> know, but to remind them of what they already know...be-
> cause even though they are so widely known and their truth
> is so obvious to everyone, they are just as widely ignored
> and forgotten.

Henny Youngman's quip, that "the secret of a happy marriage remains a secret,"
is cute but incorrect.

Torah students know the "secrets": good *middos* (*derech eretz kadma l'Torah*,
"civil, polite behavior comes before Torah!").[1] This is why boys are advised to study
Torah first and only "*afterward* take a wife"[2] (as Yaakov did, by spending fourteen
years in the yeshiva of Shem preparing for marriage).[3]

This book, a surface guide to marital *tikun hamiddos* and laying strong foundations for a *bayis ne'eman b'Yisroel* (a faithful Jewish home), is intended to give
you a glimpse into those open "secrets," despite the fact that, in Luzzato's opinion,
"they are so widely known and their truth is so obvious to everyone, [yet] they are
just as widely ignored and forgotten!"

---

1.   *Vayikra Rabba.*
2.   *Kiddushin* 29b.
3.   Rashi, *Bereishis* 28:9.

Introduction

Shalom Bias

In December 2007, a news report out of Mississippi interviewed a man whose wedding ring deflected a bullet and saved his life when his antique shop was robbed.

"I knew being married was a good thing," he told ABC News. "I just didn't know it was that good!"

Traditionally, the word *shalom* means "peace," and *shleimus* means "being complete."

The two go hand in hand. Remove *shleimus* from *shalom* and you get not peace but merely the absence of conflict, hostility and tension. Merge the two and you get a "wholesome" peace with harmony.[1]

The expression *shalom bayis* thus means a home not just "at peace" but a home that is "in agreement" with itself (i.e., *shalom bayis*, not *shalom* bias!).

This is the type of home in which the *Shechina* itself – God's Presence – prefers to dwell (as the Gemora says, *ish v'isha zachu, Shechina shruya beineihem*, "a man and a woman who are worthy [i.e., they have peace between them], the *Shechina* rests between them"[2]). "How goodly are your tents, O Yaakov!"[3]

Of course this type of perfected "domestic bliss" doesn't just happen; it

---

1. *Midrash Tanchuma Tzav* 7; *Shoftim* 18; *Meshech Chochma* to *Bereishis* 14:29.
2. *Sota* 17a.
3. *Bamidbar* 24:5.

requires hard work, lots of *seichel* (smarts), and a dose of psychology from both sides, forming a joint familial task force which, when it performs well, is credited by the Torah as being equal to one who brings harmony and peace to the entire nation of Israel.[4]

The lyrics of *Tehillim* (Psalms) remind us that Jews are not only to "seek" peace, but to "pursue" it.[5] How far should one go? Yeshayahu (Isaiah) replies, "To the far and to the near!"

In other words, "seek" peace at the place where you are, and if you do not find it there, "pursue" it in other places![6]

Parents bless their children *erev Shabbas* with peace, a theme borrowed from *Birkas Kohanim* (the priestly blessing), a blessing that God instructs Moshe to teach Aaron (which also appears at the end of both the *Shemoneh Esrei* and *Birkas Hamazon*, the central prayer of the thrice-daily prayer service and the grace after meals, respectively).

According to *Ha'amek Davar*, a nineteenth-century commentary, this three-part blessing is in ascending order, with peace being the highest blessing God and parents can bestow upon their nation and children:

> May *Hashem* bless you and keep you!
> May *Hashem* deal kindly and graciously with you!
> May *Hashem* bestow favor upon you and grant you peace
> (*v'yaseim l'cha shalom*)![7]

Sifra, a midrashic collection, bluntly comments on the Torah blessing "And you shall eat your bread to the full…and I will give peace in the land"[8] by adding that without peace "food and drink is worth nothing!"

Those who achieve true *shalom bayis* are the beneficiaries of a unique Godly blessing, based on a Mishna rule that "Peace is the vessel that holds and sustains God's blessing."[9]

---

4. *Avos d'Rabbi Nosson* 28.
5. *Tehillim* 34:15.
6. *Yeshayahu* 57:19.
7. *Bamidbar* 6:24–26.
8. *Vayikra* 26:3–6.
9. *Uktzin* 3:12. *Shalom* (peace) appears twenty-five times in the Torah. Jewish mystics note that the *gematria* (numerical value) of the word *ko*, in the Torah verse directed at the *kohanim*, "*Ko sevarchu* (So you shall bless)," is also twenty-five, suggesting that the greatest blessing is that of peace (*Zohar* 1:90).

Tranquility and wholesomeness are the rewards of what the Midrash calls a *gadol hashalom*, "the greatest-is-peace" ideology:[10] contented children, raised to the *chuppa* and *chesed*, are the byproduct.

When asked what factors produced good children, the Steipler Rav listed two: prayer and *shalom bayis*, the twin sources of all blessings.

"The greater the harmony, mutual respect and devotion between a husband and wife," wrote the seventh Rebbe of Chabad, "the greater is the measure of God's blessings to both of them for all their needs."

Commenting on the Talmud's observation that "a proper match is as difficult as the splitting of the sea," Rabbi Yehuda Loew, the Maharal of Prague, added that the miracle is not in finding the match, but in keeping the couple happily together for the rest of their lives!

But this is precisely why it matters so much. "The difficulty in achieving *shalom bayis*," wrote the Lubavitcher Rebbe, "is the best indicator of its vital importance."

---

10. *Bereishis Rabba; Chulin* 141a.

Tip 1:
Comedy

Tip 2:
Communication, Conversation

Tip 3:
Common Sense

Tip 4:
Compromise, Causation

Tip 5:
Caring, Compassion, Courtesy

Tip 6:
Commonality, Compatibility, Commitment

Tip 7:
Camaraderie, Companionship

Laughter is the shortest distance
between two people!

– Victor Borge

The Israeli Secret Service are interviewing three possible candidates, two men and one woman, for the position of an assassin. Shmuly comes in, sits down, and is handed a gun.

"Behind that door," says the interviewer, "is your wife. We want you to go in and shoot her."

"My wife?" Shmuly replies. "I can't do that! She's my wife!"

So he is dismissed.

Yankie then comes in, sits down, and is handed the gun.

"Behind that door," says the interviewer, pointing to another room, "is your wife. We want you to go in and shoot her."

"OK," Moishie replies, and goes into the room, but comes out right away. "Sorry, I just can't do it! She's my wife! The mother of my children!"

So he is dismissed.

Next comes in Suzy. She sits down, and is handed the gun.

"Behind that door," says the interviewer, pointing to another room, "is your husband. We want you to go in and shoot him."

"OK," she says, and goes into the room. Suddenly, the agents hear *Bang! Bang!* then some screaming, crashing, banging on the walls and several minutes of loud noises. Finally, it's all quiet. The door opens slowly and Suzy crawls out of the room, her clothes disheveled, her face and arms scratched, blood everywhere.

"What happened?" the interviewer asks her.

"Some idiot loaded this gun with blanks," she pants, wiping the sweat from her brow. "I had to beat him to death with the chair!"

Simchas Hachaim – Lighten Up!

> When Moshe met Zippora at the well, her father, Yisro, immediately suggested that he marry his daughter, despite the fact that Moshe was a total stranger, a penniless refugee, a man with no future. Why? Because when you have seven daughters, you don't ask too many questions!

You know why Pharoah was upset around the time of Moshe's birth? He was having a mid-wife crisis!

The family that laughs together…stays together!

It is essential not to take yourself too seriously, and not to make issues out of non-issues.

If you want your prospects for success in *shalom bayis* to rise dramatically, learn what to overlook, and become skilled at letting things be.

Shalom bayis requires that each spouse become disciplined at distinguishing the unimportant ("small stuff") from the important ("big stuff").

"You've got to think about 'big things' while you're doing small things," concluded Alvin Toffler, famous American futurist,[1] "so that all the small things go in the right direction."

If you stress before it's necessary to stress, you'll suffer more than it's necessary to suffer!

> "*Mazel tov, mazel tov*" the *shadchan* (matchmaker) says to the *chasan* (bridegroom). "I'm sure you'll look back and remember today as the happiest day of your life."
> "But I'm not getting married until tomorrow."
> "I know," replies the *shadchan*.

What happens in your relationship is not as important as how you react to what happens.

---

1. Quoting non-Jewish sources to support a Torah position is perfectly acceptable under the Talmudic adage "*Chochma bagoyim taamin* (that there is wisdom among the nations you should believe)," which can be loosely translated as, "If there is wisdom among the nations, you should accept it."

The challenge of *shalom bayis* is not how to manage marital stress, but how to manage yourself. Or as Mark Twain put it: "I'm an old man and I've had many troubles, most of which never happened!"

When asked to explain the reason for his longevity, a wise hundred thirteen-year-old man replied, "When it rains, I let it!"

Know when to let go. In short: don't become a "kvetcher"!

> Abie got a new dog and wants to show him off to his neighbor Sam. So he picks up a branch, throws it, and says to the dog, "Fetch!"
>
> But instead, the dog lies down and says, "My life is so boring. I'm tired, hungry, overweight. I never go out anymore. Life's a real drag!"
>
> "Hey," asks Sam, "what's going on?"
>
> Replies Abie: "He thought I said *kvetch*!"

There's no need to make a big deal out of everything. Why? As they say in French, "*La vie est dure* (life is hard)." Since life brings its own *tzores*, there's no need to import self-inflicted worries!

Here's the compelling truth: not everything is an emergency!

Don't underestimate the value of sometimes just doing nothing. "Go with the flow," as they say, in line with Abe Lincoln's reasoning: "People are as happy as they make up their minds to be!"

The pressures of life – its difficulties, hardships and obstacles – are best handled with humor.

> Leah is being interviewed at the local welfare service. "So," asks the interviewer, "how many children do you and your husband have?"
>
> "Four."
>
> "What are their names?"
>
> "Eenie, Meenie, Minie, George."
>
> "George? Why did you name your fourth child George?"
>
> "Because my husband didn't like Moe."

Remember: you don't stop laughing because you grow old; you grow old because you stopped laughing! Look at marriage as one long dessert – or just spell "stressed" backwards and you'll get…desserts!

Any worthwhile and effective *shalom bayis* stress-reduction kit would include a prescription of laughter, and this enthusiastic word of advice from *Pirkei Avos*: greet others with a *seiver panim yafos* (a cheerful countenance).[2]

Rav Shimshon Raphael Hirsch adds this *bon mot*: if others think you are genuinely friendly, they are more likely to be kindly disposed back to you (the Hebrew word for "face," *panim*, is similar to the word *pnim*, which means "interior"; a person's face reveals his inner feelings).

In his *Sefer Hamashalim* (Book of Parables), the great Sephardic Rav Yosef Gikatilla compares *simcha* (happiness) to "day" and *atzvus* (sadness) to "night," saying that *simcha* lights up a person as the sun lights up the day.

Rav Chaim Shmuelevitz, commenting on the loss of thirty-three years of Yaakov's life because of his comment to Pharaoh that the days of his life were few and bad, notes that Yaakov only said twenty-five of the thirty-three words he was punished for. Why? Because the remaining eight were Pharaoh's question, "How many are the days of the years of your life?" – a question posed because Yaakov's exterior expression was one of sorrow, not joy.

And in one of his letters, the *Chazon Ish* writes how satisfied he gets when cheering others up.[3]

Don't pull your hair out when times are tough; pull a joke out of a book instead! Teach yourself to see the the humor in humorless situations; discipline yourself to stop in the midst of a crisis and ask yourself: is this *really* a crisis? Perhaps it's more of a "Singing in the Rain" moment! Your life should always be set on the automatic good-humored pilot.

Rabbi Yitzchak Ariel of Petach Tikvah would train his young children to greet others with a smile so that it would become ingrained in their character. Each child would practice by going out, knocking on the door, and coming back in, expressing happiness at seeing his "guest" (sibling).

If Rabbi Ariel felt that their greetings were not warm enough, they had to repeat the exercise.

---

2. *Pirkei Avos* 1:15.
3. *Chazon Ish, Kovetz Igros*, vol. 1.

Hearing that her friend is not feeling well, the good-natured Estie decides to call and cheer her up. "Hi," she says on the phone, "how are you feeling?"

"Terrible. I have a bad migraine and a fever, and every bone in my body hurts. I have to stay in bed all day."

"Well, why don't I come over later, cook you dinner, and I'll put the kids to bed."

"Oh, that would be great!"

"I'll go to the market first and pick up some food. What does Moishie like to eat?"

"Moishie?"

"Yes," says Estie, "your husband."

"My husband's name is Cliff."

"Oh," says Estie, chagrined, "I'm terribly sorry! I must have the wrong number!"

There is a long pause and then the other woman says, "Does that mean you're not coming over?"

The reward for bringing joy and laughter to a bride and groom, says the *Mateh Moshe*,[4] based on a verse in *Tehillim*, is that "you will see your children's children" (i.e., longevity), which itself "brings peace to all Israel."[5]

The standard Hebrew words for happiness (*osher, simcha, hatzlacha*) do not define fun; in fact, there is no single definition of happiness in Judaism. In general, it is a Torah-based cognitive therapy that simply means living rightly, a skill that can be learned.[6]

Dale Carnegie's popular motto ("Success is getting what you want; happiness is wanting what you get") wasn't original. It was taken from *Pirkei Avos's* "*Eizehu ashir?* (Who is happy?) *Hasameiach b'chelko* (The one who is content with what he has)!"

"There is no mitzva to be *b'simcha*," according to the nineteenth-century chassidic leader Reb Aharon of Karlin, "but *simcha* can bring one to the greatest mitzvos – and there is no *aveira* (prohibition) to be *b'atzvus* (in a state of sadness) – yet *atzvus* can bring one to the greatest *aveiros*."

Inspired by the lyrics of *Tehillim* (*Ivdu es Hashem b'simcha*, "Serve God with

---

4.   *Gemilus Chasadim* 3:2.
5.   *Tehillim* 128:6.
6.   *Devarim* 26:11.

joy"),[7] Reb Nachman of Breslov, an enthusiastic advocate of enjoyment, taught his students, *"Mitzva gedola lihiyos b'simcha tamid (It is a great mitzva to be always joyous)!"*

A hundred fifty years later, Charlie Chaplin summarized that *vort* in song: "Smile, and the world smiles with you!"

As the Yiddishists would say: If your teeth are clenched and your fists are clenched, your relationship (and lifespan) are also probably clenched.

Remember: a single crust of pizza eaten in peace and happiness is better than a whole wedding banquet eaten in anxiety!

> A dietitian was addressing a large audience:
>
> "The material we put into our stomachs is enough to have killed most of us sitting here, years ago. Red meat is awful. Vegetables can be disastrous. Fried food is bad. But there is one thing that is the most dangerous of all, and yet all of us eat it. Can anyone here tell me what lethal product I'm referring to?"
>
> A little old Jewish man in the front row raises his hand.
>
> "Yes, sir, what do you think is the most dangerous of foods?"
>
> "Wedding cake!"

"The arrival of a good clown," wrote the seventeenth-century physician Dr. Thomas Sydenham, "exercises a more beneficial influence upon the health of a town than the arrival of twenty donkeys laden with medicine!"

Those with a healthy sense of humor have a good sense of life.

Laughter is your best friend in marriage, humor the vehicle that brightens family life. It lightens the load, eases the tension. Happy couples who laugh together last together happily. Why? Because it takes happy people to make a happy marriage.

If you have to weep, goes the old Yiddish saying, "weep before God – and laugh before people."

"Common sense (i.e., *seichel*) and a sense of humor are the same thing moving at different speeds," wrote William James, leading American philosopher. "A sense of humor is just common sense, dancing!"

---

7.   *Tehillim* 100:2.

The enduring love, wrote G.J. Nathan, famed American critic, "is the love that laughs."

Or as Victor Borge, the brilliant Danish-American humorist and pianist, put it: laughter is the shortest distance between two people!

> The newly married yeshiva couple are driving from Boro Park to Toronto for a family wedding and get stopped at the border.
>
> "Purpose of visit?" asks a customs agent.
>
> "We're going to a wedding," the wife replies.
>
> "Are you carrying any weapons – knives, guns, ammunition?"
>
> "No," the husband replies, "it's not that kind of wedding."

A person's cheer level is about half genetic, scientists say. So everyone has a good head start. The rest is up to you. And "the one who finds it hardest to be happy," notes Rabbi Manis Friedman, "is the one who needs to be happy the most!"

Shalom bayis is a beneficiary of this "positive psychology" attitude where the essence lies in the will. Remember: it's life, liberty, and the *pursuit* of happiness – not the *purchase* of happiness ("Whoever said money can't buy happiness isn't spending it right," proclaims a Lexus ad).

Yes, fiscal fitness and feeling fine are often synonymous, but just as often, not. "Gross national happiness," declared the King of Bhutan, "is more important than gross national product."

The art of *shalom bayis* is like any art: the more you practice it, the better you get at it!

But, despite the popular saying, practice does not make perfect; practice makes you perfect, *briefly*. Marital harmony requires a sustained, regular, ongoing practice. The correct saying is: Practice, practice, and more practice…makes one perfect.

The happiest couples make it a point to surround themselves with happy family members and friends, don't care about keeping up with the Cohens next door, appreciate what they have, emphasize each other's strengths instead of their weaknesses, judge themselves by their own yardsticks, never against what others do or have, and, most importantly, the humble happiness *maven* gives charity quietly and forgives easily.

> A visiting tourist from Tel Aviv walks up to a jazz musician playing the saxophone on a street corner in Manhattan, and asks, "Excuse me. How do I get to Carnegie Hall?"
>
> The saxophonist stops playing, looks up and says, "Practice, man, practice!"

Chassidus teaches: *simcha* is an attitude, a state of mind, a way of being. Even if there is no reason to smile, adds Rebbetzin Esther Jungreis, "smile anyway and God will give you a reason!" (Remember: the smallest, easiest, least expensive kindness you can do for another is to smile.)

Writing about laughter in the science section of the *New York Times*,[8] John Tierney notes, "It's not about getting the joke. It's about getting along!"

Laughter helps spouses get through the thick and thin of daily married life. It reduces the strain that lurks in every relationship. How does it help *shalom bayis*? It eases tension, releases emotions, provides a calmer atmosphere…and it's cheaper (and more effective) than psychotherapy.

A good sense of humor, which is the strongest weapon against adversity, will not only keep everybody lighthearted – because it decreases "stress" hormones and relaxes the muscles – but it gives a level of resilience that helps deal with hardship and pain by creating a general, contagious sense of well-being.

Laughter allows you to be who you are. Humor helps you react to things naturally. It makes you a calmer, better-balanced spouse.

> Rivka went to her doctor for a checkup. Afterwards, the doctor said to her, "I must inform you that you have a fissure in your uterus, and if you ever have a baby it would be a miracle."
>
> As soon as she got home, Rivka said to her husband, "You vouldn't belief it. I vent to the doctah and he told me, 'You haf a fish in your uterus and if you haf a baby it vill be a mackerel!'"

Is humor therapy found in rabbinic texts? Absolutely.

---

8. March 13, 2007.

From *Mishlei* (Proverbs) we get this gem: "A cheerful heart is a good medicine [whereas] a downcast spirit dries up the bones."[9]

When asked how a certain patient could be healed quicker, the fourteenth-century French surgeon Henri de Mondeville replied, "Allow his relatives and special friends to cheer him – and have someone tell him jokes!" (Incidentally, why do we read from a Haggada? Because we want to be able to Seder right words!)

In a study published in the *Journal of Holistic Nursing*, patients were told one-liners after surgery and before painful medication. Those exposed to humor perceived less pain as compared to patients who didn't get a dose of humor as part of their therapy.

In his famous book *Anatomy of an Illness*, longtime editor of the *Saturday Review* Norman Cousins details how he used laughter to help ease his pain while undergoing treatment for spinal rheumatoid arthritis.

When Dr. Michael R. Wasserman came down with pneumonia, he "pulled out videotapes of *I Love Lucy* reruns and laughed myself back to good health. Clearly, humor and laughter have a positive effect on one's attitude."

> Howard comes home from work and finds his wife crying hysterically in the kitchen.
>
> "What happened?" he asks her.
>
> "I decided we should eat in for a change so I cooked us a special dinner – but the dog ate it!"
>
> "Don't worry, honey," he comforts her. "I'll get you another dog."

The story is told how Reb Simcha Bunim of Peshischa once saw a man drowning in the Baltic waters, his arms flailing around in fear and panic. It was impossible to reach the man in time to save him, so Reb Simcha tried laughter, shouting to the man, "Give my regards to the Leviathan!"

The man began to laugh, regained his composure, his fear decreased, and he was able to hold out until help arrived.

Laughing is like aerobics; it provides a healthy workout before tackling life's issues.

---

9.   *Mishlei* 17:22.

> On a vacation drive to Canada, the wife's brain is working
> overtime trying to convert centigrade to Fahrenheit, Cana-
> dian dollars to American dollars, and kilometers to miles. As
> they drive by a sign that says, "Population 49,000," she turns
> to her husband and asks, "How many is that in Americans?"

When faced with anxiety, smile first. That's what the First Couple of Judaism
did.

When informed by God that he would father a child in his elderly years,
Avraham responded with laughter; when Sarah found out, how did she respond?
With a chuckle, *twice!*[10] Both laughed together – albeit for different reasons.

God asks Sarah why she's laughing.

The first matriarch admits that it was her knee-jerk reaction to being "dismissive" and "fearful" (i.e., easing the tensions), and then she declares, "*Tz'chok asa
li Elokim, kol hashomea yitzchak li* (God has made laughter for me; all who hear
will laughingly rejoice over me!)."[11] Similarly, the writer of *Tehillim* sings, "Then
our mouths shall be filled with laughter, and our tongues with song!"[12]

It is God Himself who suggests the name Yitzchak[13] for Judaism's first baby
boy.

The Hebrew root of Yitzchak (*tzadi-chet-koof*) means "laughter," and refers
to the joy that the baby brought to his childless mother.[14]

---

10. *Bereishis* 18:12, 21:6.
11. *Bereishis* 21:6.
12. *Tehillim* 126:2.
13. *Bereishis* 17:17–19.
14. As a warning that clowning around can be serious business, the Torah uses the same
    Hebrew root letters when the Jews make a golden calf, celebrate with food and drink,
    and then *l'tzachek* (make merry). When Lot warns his sons-in-law to get out of Sodom,
    it is "a joke in their eyes," and they suffer the same destruction. The Talmud has a thread
    weaving through it which can be summarized as: Curb your joy! This is based on the
    Torah admonition to "rejoice with trepidation" (*Tehillim* 2:11; *Brachos* 30b–31a). Rabba
    and Rabbi Zeira warned their students Abaye and Rabbi Yirmiya not to be so excessively
    cheerful. "We are wearing *tefillin*," they replied, which made it OK. In three different
    wedding tales in the Talmud, Mar ben Ravina, Rav Ashi, and Rav Hamnuna Zuti en-
    sured that the *leibedig simcha* didn't get too carried away (the first two broke precious
    cutlery amidst the dancing, the third introduced a solemn theme in his *drasha*). When
    Rabbi Yochanan quoted Shimon bar Yochai ("It is forbidden to fill our mouths with
    laughter in this world"), his student-colleague, Reish Lakish, took this literally – and
    never laughed again!

Rashi explains the difference between the two laughters: Avraham laughed because he believed God and was rejoicing, but Sarah, instead of a heartfelt "From-your-lips-to-God's-ears!" response, laughed in disbelief, dismissive, scoffing.[15]

This is why God asks Sarah, and not Avraham, "Why did you laugh?"

Saadia Gaon explains why: laughter is the reaction people have to a sudden realization of an underlying truth. Rav Shimshon Raphael Hirsch adds that laughter results from sudden contrasts, from pairing incompatible objects. This is why Purim is Judaism's official annual Day of Laughter: Jews went from being the target of annihilation to being heroes and victors, erupting in the laughter of relief.

> The elderly Jewish woman goes to the doctor's office. After a few minutes in the examination room, she bolts out, screaming as she runs down the hall. The doctor's partner stops her and asks her what happened. He then barges into the doctor's room and says, "Are you crazy? Mrs. Cohen is seventy-three years old, has five grown children and twenty-one grandchildren – and you tell her she is pregnant?!"
>
> "Yep," the doctor replies, and smiles. "Sure cured her hiccups though, didn't it?"

To emphasize the importance of the human trait of "being happy," the Jewish calendar ends the year with the month of Adar, a month of mandatory joy, kicked off by the theme of Purim.

The expression *Pachad Yitzchak*, "the Fear of Isaac," which literally means "fear will laugh" (after the fear of Haman's genocide was overturned, the mood turned to joy), acknowledges that humor is a powerful emotion that releases stress, tension and trauma.

The Lubavitcher Rebbe would point out that there are only two Torah readings (*parshios*) that begin with the words "These are the *toldos* (offspring) of…" One is "These are the *toldos* of Noah," and another begins, "These are the *toldos* of Yitzchak."[16]

The former *parsha* is called *Noach*, the latter simply *Toldos*. Why doesn't it mention Yitzchak's name? Because the story of Noah's life is the story of one life; but Yitzchak's story, with the connotation of joy, is the story of Jewish life itself.

---

15.   *Targum Onkelos*, Rashi, *Bereishis* 17:17.
16.   *Bereishis* 6:9, 25:19.

Fast forward two thousand years after Avraham to the Talmud and we see the tradition of Jewish merrymaking still around. The great sage Rabba would not begin a *shiur* without a joke. Why? Because a good joke opens the mind to serious learning.

Rabbi Dov Ber of Mezritch, disciple of the Baal Shem Tov, extended the Talmud's recommendation of a joke before Torah study and applied it to prayer, so as to pray with a joyful expanded consciousness. (What do you call a Torah with a seat belt? A *sefer Torah*!)

One day, just before *Shacharis*, he organized a practical joke on one of his chassidim. When the room was convulsed in laughter, he yelled out, "OK! Now let's pray!"

> The paper bag is in terrible pain, so he goes to see a doctor.
> "I'm afraid your condition is incurable," the physician says.
> "Oh, no! How did I catch this?"
> "It's genetic. Your grandfather was a carrier!"

An ancient kabbalistic text compiled by Rabbi Akiva links each Jewish month to a Hebrew letter and a particular organ or sense of the body. Adar is linked to *kof*, "laughter," and the organ is the spleen (*techol*), considered the controller of the sense of laughter. Ironically, the spleen is considered the seat of *mara shechora*, "black humor" (depression, despair), but the same Hebrew letters of *mara shechora* spell out *hirhur sameiach*, "a happy thought"!

And by making Adar the only month in a leap year that repeats itself (seven times every nineteen years), we show that, at the end of the year, laughter is the only one of the twelve human senses that should overflow in our lives.

Noting that two months of Adar is sixty days, Jewish mystics tie it to the halacha that a formula of sixty-to-one in dietary laws is a nullifying ratio. Thus, sixty days of laughter has the power to nullify any bitterness from the preceding year.

But remember: happiness in marriage is not a gift, but an opportunity to make *others* happy; it's an obligation, not an experiment!

And part of the mitzva of *simchas chassan v'kalla*, "joy of groom and bride," is "*Keitzad merakdin lifnei hakalla?* (How do we dance before the bride?)," the talmudic discussion of appropriate merrymaking at a wedding which describes making *others* dance and have fun.[17] This is how the idea of a *badchan* (jester) started. His job? Make the guests merry by standing on a table and telling rhymed jokes that interweave scriptural verses in order to poke gentle fun at prominent attendees.

Many prominent chassidic rebbes and Torah scholars (e.g., Rabbi Mordechai Rackover, the Ropshitzer, Reb Naftali, disciple of Rebbe Yaakov Yitzhak, the Seer of Lublin, etc.), who read the tales of Chelm and had time to laugh at the antics of Hershele Ostropoler, were themselves *badchanim*, convinced that the pursuit of humor was a spiritual path.

> The newlywed husband walks into a psychiatrist's office. "Doc, every time I see my wife take out nickels, dimes and quarters from her wallet, I have a panic attack! What's the problem with me?"
>
> "Oh," replies the doctor, "it's obvious. You're just afraid of change!"

The armor of *shalom bayis* is humor, its weapon the spontaneous smile.

"If I look sad when I walk in a room, what happens to the person sitting next to me? He feels a bit uncomfortable," writes Shlomo Carlebach. "When you smile, filled with joy, and you look at somebody, they look back at you. When you cry they can't really look back at you. You can smile eye to eye – but you can't cry eye to eye!"

"You cannot be mad at somebody who makes you laugh," says the late-night philosopher Jay Leno, "it's as simple as that!" Adds Bob Newhart: "Laughter gives us distance. It allows us to step back from an event, deal with it and then move on!"

Problems in relationships are half solved if you find the humor in them. Remember: frowns are also contagious.

Surround yourself with friends who smile and fill the house with an air of upbeat expectations. Family arguments, in this atmosphere, seem less weighty, more congenial to solutions.

Discipline yourself and your spouse to react to worries with the sigh of a smile. This attitude will help you avoid fighting over trivia and minutia, and will help you determine what's significant and what's petty, frivolous, inconsequential.

Of course, this doesn't give you a license to be cavalier in your marriage.

---

17.   *Chochmas Manoach, Kesubos* 17a.

Maturity and *seichel* demand that, in the style of *Koheles*, you know when to laugh, when not to.

> The cute little girl goes into a pet store and asks the salesgirl, "Do you sell little rabbits?"
>
> "Of course we do," the salesgirl replies, bending down and patting the cute little girl on the head, "We have a sweet little black bunny, a friendly brown bunny with long ears, and a very lovable white bunny. Which would you prefer?"
>
> "No matter," the cute little girl replies, "I don't think my python cares what color it is!"

Laughing together with your spouse is a way of connecting; a keen sense of humor makes it healthier for you to cope with challenges.

How will you know if you have a good sense of humor?

Frank Tyger explains, "The ultimate test of whether you possess a sense of humor is your reaction when someone tells you you don't!"

The Torah advises Jews to smile as part of our genetic makeup. Thus you should instill it in your children at a young age, nurture it through their childhood and encourage it in their teenage years.

Shalom bayis breathes easier in the presence of children who have a well-developed sense of humor.

This doesn't mean you have to fake slipping on a banana peel when you get home or perform a slapstick stand-up comedy routine in the living room, but it does mean that you must be constantly aware that your persona, whether happy or sad, sets the tone for the Torah household. And more: self-deprecating humor encourages the *midda* of humility.

> Mimi is stopped by an usher at the entrance to the synagogue hall who says, "Wait a minute! Are you a friend of the bride?"
>
> "No, of course not!" she replies, "I'm the groom's mother!"

The *Reader's Digest* got it right: laughter *is* the best medicine.

If you're going to start unpacking your emotional baggage after the *chuppa*, a humor-rich environment becomes critical; the family funny bone will soon loom as *shalom bayis's* most underestimated armor.

Tehillim recognizes it as it sings *Ul'yishrei lev simcha,* those with a "straight heart [have] *simcha,*" the joy expressed in laughter. Rabbi Moshe Alshich, the great Turkish preacher of the sixteenth century who lived in Safed, adds, "Words that come out of the heart enter into the heart."

During the Civil War, President Abraham Lincoln interrupted a meeting by reading an amusing story. But no one smiled. Finally, Lincoln said, "Gentlemen, why don't you laugh? With the fearful strain that is upon me day and night, if I did not laugh I should die, and you need this medicine as much as I do!"

> Chani and Yankie are on vacation in Italy when they come across a wishing well. Yankie leans over, makes a wish and throws in a dime. Chani then decides to make a wish, too, but she leans over too much, loses her balance, and falls into the well.
>
> Yankie, stunned, smiles broadly and says, "Wow! It really works!"

So take time to share jokes, play games, learn to laugh at yourself.

If you lose your sense of humor, you lose your footing. If you lose your grounding in what issues are – or aren't – serious – you chip away at the foundations of *shalom bayis.* The "peace" in the home begins to fracture. The going gets tough, and, without the tools of humor and *seichel,* it's inevitable that an abyss of despair, stress and anxiety, all mortal enemies of *shalom bayis,* will surreptitiously enter the home.

Life then becomes not a steady, sane path but a slippery tightrope.

Humor helps us keep our balance, reduces stress and puts problems into perspective.

It replaces helplessness with immediate hope (when the condemned man was asked by the head of the firing squad if he wanted a last cigarette, the prisoner replied, "No, thanks, I'm trying to quit smoking!").

And most important: it helps lightens the burden of those around you!

Rav Rafoel Levin on the Obligatory Smile

One day a distraught couple came to Rav Rafoel Levin asking for a divorce. Rav Rafoel, brother-in-law of Rav Yosef Shalom Elyashiv, was reluctant and preferred to resurrect the *shalom bayis* that once existed.

So he turned to the husband, and said, "It is an accepted practice for a sick person to have a new name added, via the process of *shinui hasheim*. This new name brings *mazel* and, hopefully, helps the patient. But it needs to last thirty days, so I'd like you to give your wife a new name and, for the next thirty days, greet her that way with a smile and with terms of endearment."

The couple followed the rav's suggestion and, within a month, had restored calm to the household and no longer wanted a divorce. It was the repeating of his wife's name in a gentle tone and smile that turned things around in their relationship.

The Secret of Happiness

In the olden days there was a tribe always at war with other tribes. They seemed to have no morals, love or compassion – only a death wish. So the elders of the other tribes got together to find a way to save the angry tribe from themselves. They decided to take the secret of contentment and happiness away from those who abused it and hide it from them. But where should this secret be hidden? Some suggested it be buried deep underground; others said hide it on top of the highest mountain; still others thought the secret should be thrown into the deepest ocean. They couldn't agree, until the Elder made the decision: "Let us hide the secret within the people themselves. People like this will never find happiness and contentment there."

And to this day people have been feverishly pursuing the secret of life's contentment and happiness, few ever finding its hiding place – already within themselves!

Eliyahu Hanavi on Humor

Rabbi Broka Hoza'a was often in the market at Bai Lepat where Eliyahu Hanavi spoke to him. Each day, he asked Eliyahu, "Is there anyone here who has *olam haba* (the eternal world)?" to which Eliyahu's reply repeatedly was, "No."

One day, Eliyahu said, "Those two."

Rabbi Broka ran over and excitedly asked them, "What [special thing] do you do?" They answered, "We're comedians. We cheer up depressed people..."

– Taanis 22a

Like His Mother Used to Do

My husband didn't like my pudding
And he didn't like my cake.
My biscuits were too hard.
Not like his mother used to bake.

I didn't perk the coffee
And I didn't make the stew,
I didn't mend his socks
Like his mother used to do.

As I pondered for an answer
I was looking for a clue.
So, I turned around and boxed his ears,
Like his mother used to do.

To Build a Bridge

"There was a city that had two very high mountains and a very deep valley between them with gushing water. A potential fall from the mountain would be absolutely lethal. The king of the city declared that anyone who succeeded in building a bridge between the mountains would be rewarded with great wealth and would be made second to the king. However, there was one condition: the builder would have to build himself a house on the bridge and live there for the rest of his life to guarantee the safety of the bridge at all times. The king wanted to be certain that the builder would reinforce the bridge with solid foundations that would last forever.

"So it is with a marriage," concluded Rav Lopian. "The bond between a husband and wife is a wonderful and truly beneficial thing. However, in order for it to last forever – in order for both spouses to overcome the bumps along the way – they need all the reinforcement they can get. Therefore, it is our job to gladden them and encourage them as they go to build a new home in the Jewish nation."

– Rav Eliyahu Lopian, speaking at a wedding celebration, explaining why our Sages stress the importance of gladdening a *chasan* and *kalla*

Rav Aaron Kotler Sets an Example

A *talmid* of Rav Aaron Kotler recalls once driving the *rosh yeshiva* to Lakewood from his home in Boro Park. Reb Aaron was already seated in the car when he suddenly excused himself and asked the driver if he would mind waiting a moment while he took care of something in his house. The *talmid* followed the *rosh yeshiva* up to his third-floor apartment to be of assistance if necessary. They entered the apartment, and Reb Aaron went to his *rebbetzin*, wished her "*A gutten tag*," turned around and left.

In his haste, it seems, he had left the house without bidding her good-bye. The *talmid* says that to this day he remembers the glow of pleasure that lit up the *rebbetzin*'s face because of this simple gesture.

The *Rosh Yeshiva* of Telz Takes Out the Garbage

It is told that a couple once complained of their *shalom bayis* problems to Rav Mordechai Gifter, the *rosh yeshiva* of Telz. The wife mentioned that her husband refused to take out the garbage, claiming that as a *ben Torah* it was not fitting. The *rav* ruled that this was correct and the husband left feeling very satisfied.[18]

The very next morning, bright and early, there was a knock at the couple's door. The husband opened it and was shocked to see the *rosh yeshiva* himself. "Wh-what," the husband stammered, "what brings Moreinu HaRav to our home this morning?" The *rosh yeshiva* replied with a smile, "You probably have garbage to take out. I am not a *ben Torah* so I'll do it for you."

The husband was so embarrassed he got the point.

---

18. In fact, the Rambam writes that removing the garbage, washing oneself, having clean clothes, etc., are all Torah values (*Moreh Nevuchim* 3:34). Rav Shlomo Zalman Auerbach's clothes were always spotless and his shoes always polished. He took such good care of his hat and his glasses that he wore the same ones for decades.

Tip 1: Comedy

Tip 2: Communication, Conversation

Tip 3:
Common Sense

Tip 4:
Compromise, Causation

Tip 5:
Caring, Compassion, Courtesy

Tip 6:
Commonality, Compatibility, Commitment

Tip 7:
Camaraderie, Companionship

My wife says I never listen to her.
At least I think that's what she said!

A judge was interviewing a woman regarding her pending divorce, and asked, "What are the grounds for your divorce?"

She replied, "About four acres and a nice little home in the middle of the property with a stream running by."

"No," he said, "I mean what is the foundation of this case?"

"It is made of concrete, brick and mortar," she responded.

"I mean," he continued, "What are your relations like?"

"I have an aunt and uncle living here in town, and so do my husband's parents."

He said, "Do you have a real grudge?"

"No," she replied, "We have a two-car carport and have never really needed one."

"Please," he tried again, "is there any infidelity in your marriage?"

"Yes, both my son and daughter have stereo sets. We don't necessarily like the music, but the answer to your questions is yes."

"Ma'am, does your husband ever beat you up?"

"Yes," she responded, "about twice a week he gets up earlier than I do."

Finally, in frustration, the judge asked, "Lady, why do you want a divorce?"

"Oh, I don't want a divorce," she replied. "I've never wanted a divorce. My husband does. He says he can't communicate with me."

... peace at the place he lived ... Beit, and if you do not ...

... Yerubels Moshe to ... Etz and Bircas ... and the grace after ...

... Ibn Ezra, a noted ... commentary, this three ... the highest blessing God ...

... your peace ...

Sifra ... Num. bluntly comments on the Torah blessing "And you shall ... that the full ... and I will give peace in the land" by adding that without peace ... food and drink is worth nothing!

Those who live true *shalom bayis* are the beneficiaries of a unique Godly blessing, echoing a Mishna rule that "Peace is the vessel that holds and sustains God's blessing."

4. ... Simon 18.
5. Za...
6. *Yeshayahu* ...
7. *Bamidbar* 6:...-26
8. *Vayikra* 26:3-6
9. *Uktzin* 3:12. *Shalom* (peace) appears twenty-five times in the Torah. Jewish mystics note that the gematria (numerical value) of the word *ko*, in the Torah verse directed at the *kohanim*, "*Ko sevarchu* (So you shall bless)," is also twenty-five, suggesting that the greatest blessing is that of peace (*Zohar* 1:90).

Learn to Talk – and Listen!

> A little girl approaches a little boy in day care and says, "Hey, wanna play house?"
> "Sure! What do you want me to do?"
> "I want you to communicate."
> "Uh, that word is too big. I have no idea what it means."
> "Perfect! You can be the husband!"

A scientific study revealed that only 7 percent of communication was achieved through words, 38 percent through tonality (i.e., voice, emotion), and 55 percent through physiology (i.e., body language, gestures, facial expression).

In a fascinating Talmud, Rabbi Yehuda Hanasi, the compiler of the Mishna, responds to a halachic question from a student in very concise language.[1] But the brief response is ambiguous, and could be interpreted either strictly or leniently. What to do?

The Talmud decides based not on the words but on Rebbi's *tone* of voice: did he sound angry or gentle? It was soft-spoken. Thus, since his response was given in a tone of gentleness ("A soft reply will undo fury"),[2] the conclusion is that his answer was lenient. The lesson? Tone alone can determine a legal verdict!

Remember: in marriage, communication is not just by language.

Responses are also triggered by tone, emotions, facial expressions, body gestures (once when I had laryngitis, my wife and I worked out how to communicate through a system of taps; one tap meant "Yes," two taps meant "No," and two hundred taps was for "Take out the garbage!").

---

1.   *Zevachim* 30b.
2.   *Mishlei* 15:1.

> Sammy and Sarah are fighting and giving each other the silent treatment. One night, Sammy realizes that he needs his wife to wake him at 5:00 a.m. for an early morning business flight so, not wanting to be the first to break the silence, he leaves her a note: "Please wake me at 5:00 a.m."
>
> The next morning, Sammy wakes up and is shocked to discover it's 8:00a.m. and he has missed his flight. Next to his pillow, he finds a note from his wife: "It's 5:00 a.m. Wake up!"

The umbrella of *shalom bayis* covers homes wherein each side sees the other as an ally, not an adversary.

To live in a state of harmony, you need a passport of communication; without it you'll live in a perpetual state of conflict. Remember: anger is only one letter short of danger! Angry outbursts are not creative expressions. Instead, Mr. and Mrs. Broigess,[3] agree to disagree agreeably!

In order to build a stable, permanent home of *shalom bayis*, making the family atmosphere a safe harbor, the matrix of tenderness, tranquility and togetherness, the Talmud warns, "Do not introduce strife into your home," and, add the Sages, make sure your forgiving is as "soft as a reed, not hard as a cedar!"[4]

Since Monday, the second day of Creation, is the day of the week that introduced strife into the world, the chapter of Tehillim we say on Mondays[5] was composed by the sons of Korach, the master of confrontation, who distanced themselves from their father's rebellion.

One of the three things that God hates (the other two are anger and drunkenness) is those who demand getting their own way; another Gemora raises the stakes: those who are not demanding and those who never get angry in their own home are assured to live longer.[6]

And so Rav Ada bar Ahava, when asked to explain his extraordinary longev-

---

3.   *Broigess* means "offended" in Yiddish.

4.   *Avos* 2:15; *Yevamos* 44a, 65b; *Taanis* 20a; *Megilla* 28a; *Orach Chaim* 606:1; Rambam, *Hilchos Teshuva* 2:10; *Sefer Hachinuch* 364, 453.

5.   *Tehillim* 48:2.

6.   *Pesachim* 113b; *Rosh Hashana* 17a; *Taanis* 20b.

ity, replied, "I was never stern within my house."[7] When asked the same question, Rabbi Praida attributed it to his patience with others.[8]

"*Lo sa'aneh al riv* (Do not answer in an argument),"[9] admonishes the Torah, concerned that a retort to an insult can only lead to further antagonism, squabbling, bickering.

Chisda, the Babylonian Sage, compared anger in the house to "a worm in a plant."[10]

The person who is rapid to anger and slow to appeasement is evil, warns the Talmud, and the person who is slow to anger and rapid to appeasement is pious.[11]

Dissension in a house? It surely will lead to its destruction![12] Adds the *Zohar*: quarrelsome people soon "come to grief!"[13]

Jonathan ben Eleazar was blunt: loss of temper leads to hell! – and since, according to Rabba bar Huna, it's disrespectful to the Divine Presence,[14] it strikes a direct blow to the senior of the three partners to *shalom bayis*.

Remember: the most important rest you can take in a marriage is that moment between two deep breaths!

> At his fiftieth wedding anniversary party, the husband was asked the secret of his longevity. "Well," he replied, "when we got married we agreed that if we ever got into a fight, I would just put on my hat and go for a walk. After a while, I would return and throw my hat through the doorway. If my wife threw it back out, I went on with my walk. So I account my longevity to all the exercise I've gotten over the years!"

---

7.   *Taanis* 20b.
8.   *Eruvin* 54b.
9.   *Shemos* 23:2; *Sefer Charedim* 4.
10. *Sota* 3b.
11. *Pirkei Avos* 5.
12. *Derech Eretz Zuta* 7:37.
13. *Zohar, Bereishis* 76b.
14. *Nedarim* 22a, b.

"Many quarrels begin with legitimate disagreements," said Reb Meir Simcha of Dvinsk, but if allowed to continue they eventually take on a life of their own, so that those involved cannot even remember what the original argument was about.

> We can see this from the argument between the shepherds of Avraham and Lot. At first, the quarrel was based on the fact that there was not enough grazing land for all their herds. In time, however, the Torah tells us, they "were unable to live together," without any legitimate reason for their quarrel.

Commenting on the conflict of neighbors Avraham and Avimelech, king of Gerar,[15] the eighteenth-century Turkish Rabbi Ya'akov Kuli, in the most popular Ladino sefer ever (his commentary on the Torah, *Me'am Lo'ez*), examines their remarkable peace agreement and credits their ability to recognize each other's position: "Know that when two people have had a disagreement and wish to make peace, they must completely resolve everything that stands between them, so that they can purify their hearts. For unless each of them removes from himself whatever anger he has against the other in his heart, even though you may see them embracing, this peace is not lasting, and at the first moment of discord their hatred will easily return."

Nothing good ever comes out of controversy, warns the Midrash,[16] while *Sefer Chassidim* notes that every quarrel ends the same way: with regret.

The best response to insult, says Rashi, is to keep quiet. The Talmud turns the table against the insulter: "If your fellow calls you a donkey [it's best] to wear a saddle on your back!"[17]

In commenting on why the Torah mentions frogs ten times during the plague of frogs in Egypt, the Abarbanel says that this one plague equaled all ten plagues. Why? Because the constant croaking made life unbearable.

---

15.   *Bereishis* 20:1–8.
16.   *Sifrei, Ki Seitzei* 86.
17.   *Bava Kamma* 92b.

Similarly, no marriage can withstand the noise and disruption that come with a consistently argumentative spouse.

The Eastern European Yiddishists were blunt: Better a dry morsel and peace than a house full of feasting with strife![18]

> Benji complains to his *chaver*, "I can't take it anymore."
>
> "What's wrong?"
>
> "It's my wife. Every time we have an argument, she gets historical!"
>
> "You mean hysterical."
>
> "No, I mean historical! Every argument we have, she'll say, 'I still remember that time when you...'"

It's obvious: peace cannot reign in a domicile of domestic discord.

Ill-temper and *shalom bayis* are totally incompatible. Rage is a time bomb waiting to go off, a strong indicator that failure is just around the corner.[19]

And remember: abusive behavior is never private. You can shut the shutters but it won't help, for even "the stones and beams of a man's house testify against him!"[20]

"Hard-heartedness and temper are unworthy of a Jew," declared Moshe of Coucy, while one Midrash compares anger to worshipping idolatry, and another defines anger and temper in dark, ominous terms ("death's operatives"!).

"The Torah," declares the Rambam, "is insistent against bearing a grudge and remembering it, for one must erase from his mind the wrong that was done to him."[21]

Sefer Chassidim, when asked to choose between temper and modesty, warned, "Even if she is a *tzenua* (modest), he should not marry her if she is bad tempered" (the same applies if the boy is a great Torah scholar but has an uncontrollable temper).

---

18. *Mishlei* 17:1.
19. Here's some trivia: in the 1400s a law in England allowed a man to beat his wife with a stick no thicker than his thumb. Hence we have "the rule of thumb"!
20. *Habakuk* 2:11; *Chagiga* 16a.
21. *Hilchos Deios* 7:8.

The Vilna Gaon, whose hobby was math, discovered that at some point every single letter in the Hebrew alphabet appeared next to the other in the Torah, except for two: the *gimmel* and *taf*. When put together, they spell *get*, "divorce," something that God found so upsetting that He kept the letters apart.

> Rachel is confiding in her best friend that her *shalom bayis* is on the rocks. "I'm so unhappy," she confesses, "I've lost twenty pounds already."
>
> "If you're so unhappy, why don't you just leave?"
>
> "Are you crazy? I'm not leaving until I lose another ten pounds!"

The process of adjusting to another, known as *v'davak b'ishto* (and he shall cleave to his wife),[22] is one of the challenges of *shalom bayis* and human nature. The edges may get smoother over time but the ability to forgive (communication!) and forget (patience!) are prerequisites (and help explain the booming Valentine's Day industry where more than a billion greeting cards are exchanged, not counting the innumerable vehicles of communication such as flowers, candies and singing telegrams).

Rav Eliyahu Goldshmidt relates the tale of a man who was having severe marital issues because his wife was "driving him crazy." He simply had no patience for her. They got divorced. Some time later, Rav Goldshmidt met him and asked how things were going. "Great, I am happily remarried."

"Really? Is your second wife that much easier to deal with than your first?"

"No, not at all. In fact, she requires much more patience than my first wife."

"So, how is it that you are now happily married and having more success in being patient?"

"Simple: I learned my lesson!"

In other words: don't panic easily. It's normal that the rough edges of each personality will create friction, for "just as no two faces are alike," reminds the Talmud, "so are no two minds alike!"[23]

This is hinted at with the introduction of Eve to Adam and the Torah's use of the term *k'negdo*, a word that doesn't mean compatible but "opposite."

---

22.   *Bereishis* 2:24.
23.   *Sanhedrin* 38a.

> Sammy was on his way home one Monday but got distracted in a poker game with the boys and ended up staying out all night. When he finally showed up in the morning his wife was furious. In the midst of a heated argument, she screamed at him, "How would you like it if you didn't see me for a couple of days?"
>
> "That would suit me just fine!" Sammy shouted back.
>
> So, Tuesday came and went and he didn't see his wife. Wednesday and Thursday came and went with the same result. By Friday, the swelling went down enough so that Sammy could see his wife a little...just out of the corner of his left eye.

Ben Zoma once answered the question "Who is powerful?" with the response "He who is slow to anger."[24]

The rabbis give a clue as to how to come to really know a person: see how he or she behaves when angry![25]

According to tradition, Jewish women's greater wisdom comes from their potential as great communicators ("Ten measures of speech descended to the world," says the Talmud, "and women took nine of them"[26]).

> It was Heshie and Betty's silver wedding anniversary.
>
> "Do you remember," Betty asks her husband, "when you proposed to me? I remember that I was so overwhelmed and taken aback that I couldn't talk for a whole hour."
>
> "Of course I remember," he replies, "that was the happiest hour of my life!"

The name of the first woman, Eve (*Chava*), is related to the verb "articulate" or "express" (*mechava*), and to the word "joy" (*chedva*). Since a Jewish name conveys a person's essence, these links imply that there is a dimension of joyousness that comes through a woman's heightened capacity for expression.

Remember: your spouse is not the enemy. Don't provoke, don't become provoked. Contentiousness in the Jewish home will cause a hemorrhaging of

---

24. *Pirkei Avos* 4:1, a paraphrase of *Mishlei* 16:32.
25. *Eruvin* 65b; *Taanis* 4a; *Kiddushin* 40b–41a.
26. *Kiddushin* 49b.

shalom; it is foreign and unhealthy, and can easily be tamed with an attitude of flexibility.

Don't approach conversation just as a means to an end, but as the end itself. ("It was impossible to get a conversation going," commented that famous philosopher Yogi Berra, "'cause everybody was talking too much!")

The rabbis of the Talmud conduct a long discussion about how serious it is to pain another with hurtful words.[27]

"If one thinks honestly," wrote Rav Pesach Frank in his sefer *Shevivei Ohr*, "he realizes that when he becomes angry at another person, he causes more damage to himself than that which he may cause to his adversary. A person who is habitually angry fills his days with regret and causes himself much unnecessary anguish."

Maintaining anger produces antipathy and alienation. Antagonism towards a spouse is emotional terrorism, a psychological, profoundly destructive emotional poison.

"The only one who is harmed by a grudge," concludes Rabbi Abraham J. Twerski, "is the one who holds it – not the one against whom it is held!"

Or as the Yiddishists put it: When the kettle boils over, it pours on its own side!

> Three weeks after her wedding day, Shoshana calls her rabbi.
> "Rabbi, Rabbi, Bernie and I had a terrible fight last night, and now I don't know what to do!"
> "Calm down," the rabbi says, "it's OK. Every marriage has to have its first fight."
> "I know, I know! But I don't know where to hide the body!"

This is not to say that disputes are unnatural, even during the halcyon years. They are normal and to be expected.

Remember: "the Torah was not given to angels."[28] Thus, disagreement in marriage is to be expected; arguments and bickering are even sometimes healthy (remember: we got the name "Yisroel" only because Yaakov *fought* an angel). How did that philosopher put it? "If two people always agree, then one of them is unnecessary!"

---

27.   *Bava Metzia* 58–59.
28.   *Brachos* 25b.

"Come, now," implores Yeshayahu with the obvious "and let us reason together!"[29] As they say: Marriage is nature's way of preventing people from fighting with total strangers!

To reason with each other means keeping others out of your marital disputes. With the exception of consulting an experienced *rav*, don't involve every Tom, Dick and Harry in your domestic squabbles.

Maintaining your privacy is essential; don't share your woes with your friends or neighbors. There's an old Yiddish saying: A closed oven keeps its heat but once its door is opened the heat is lost!

Since there is hardly a house without an *idun risha*, "a moment of anger," *shalom bayis* requires not that you keep things inside you but that you know how to sensibly exit an argument – before it exits you!

In other words, good communication is Marriage 101, so control your aggression, before it controls you.

> The just-married Mendy knocks on his rabbi's door, "Can I come in?"
>
> "Of course, Mendy, come on in," the *rav* replies. "What's the problem?"
>
> "Well, it's my *shalom bayis*. My wife's crazy. I think she's trying to poison me."
>
> "Poison you? Don't be silly! You're imagining things!"
>
> "No, Rabbi, really. She's trying to poison me! What should I do?"
>
> "That's absurd, but let me talk with her anyway. I'll see what I can find out and I'll get back to you in a few days."
>
> A few days later, the *rav* calls Mendy. "Mendy, I dropped by your house yesterday and had a long conversation with your wife. You want my advice?"
>
> "Yes, Rabbi."
>
> "Take the poison!"

Before things gets out of control, remember to "fight fair," with respect, *seichel*, patience and sensitivity.

Rav Moshe Feinstein was known to have a calm nature. He never expressed

---

29. *Yeshayahu* 1:18.

any anger, even during stressful times and aggravating situations. When asked about his easygoing disposition, Rav Moshe replied, "Do you think that this is my natural instinct? On the contrary, by nature I am short-tempered, but I make a great effort to overcome my instincts."

If you insist you're right long enough, goes the Yiddish adage, you'll be wrong! In short: miscommunication can disintegrate into non-communication in no time at all!

> Sandy has an office next door to a practice of marriage coun-
> selors and one day hears lots of screaming coming from their
> offices. She goes in and asks the receptionist, "What's going
> on in there?"
>> "Oh, it's a battle of the wits."
>> "The wits?"
>> "Yeah. In that room it's Mr. and Mrs. Horowitz, and in
> the other room is Mr. and Mrs. Berkowitz!"

It's healthy to disagree (that means you are at least communicating), but make sure you manage your conflict in a responsible manner.

Disagreements don't have to spiral downwards and torpedo a relationship.

Arguments usually begin over trivial matters and then quickly escalate in the face of bruised egos; in fact, the rabbis of the Talmud urge folks not to hold it in but to "speak out and discuss the issues."[30]

The Midrash on Korach analyzes the Hebrew word for fight (*machlokes*) to reveal God's attitude to fighting between Jews. The letters of *machlokes* are *mem*, *ches, lamed, kuf, sav*. Mem (*m*) stands for *makeh* (beating), *ches* (*ch*) stands for *charon* (fury), *lamed* (*l*) stands for *likui* (punishment), *kuf* (*k*) stands for *klala* (curse) and *sav* (*t* or *s*, depending on grammatical conditions) stands for *to'eiva* (abomination). Put them all together and you see that when a Jew fights, God beats him, is furious with him, punishes him, curses him and deems him a disgusting abomination.[31]

Criticism, what we politely call "feedback," can be constructive and encouraging – or destructive and demoralizing. The former requires skill, wisdom and sensitivity. The latter can be devastating, as the case of the spies (*meraglim*)

---

30.   Rashi, *Yoma* 75a; *Mishlei* 12:25.
31.   *Bamidbar Rabba* 18.

teaches: a negative report about the Land of Israel (a "land that devours its inhabitants")[32] destroyed morale and faith and led to an entire generation of Jews being condemned to wandering the desert for forty years.[33]

And more!

Lack of communication destroyed the idyll of the Garden of Eden.

When God ordered Adam not to eat from the tree, He relied on Adam to pass it on *accurately* to Eve. When Eve was then created, Adam incorrectly and carelessly relayed the message to her, telling her God had forbidden them from *both* eating *and touching* the tree. The consequences were disastrous.

The serpent, the embodiment of the "evil inclination," seized upon the subtle difference, and pushed Eve into the tree. When she saw nothing happened from her "touching," she proceeded to eat.

If you read the opening lines of your *tenaim* ("conditions" to get married),[34]

---

32.   *Bamidbar* 13:32.

33.   *Taanis* 29a.

34.   During the Talmudic period the bride's side would give a dowry upon marriage. His family would then augment the dowry by 50 percent more than its value (*Kesubos* 67a). Both sets of parents were thus partners in the marital transaction, providing "financial backing" to the union. These arrangements were then documented in an instrument called *Shtar Pesikta*, in short, *tenaim*, "obligations" (*Kesubos* 102b; *Kiddushin* 9b). Reading the *kesuba* is a *minhag* introduced in the days of the Rishonim, "the former ones" (these were the early leading rabbis of the eleventh to fifteenth centuries) after the Geonim (the Babylonian scholars from around 589 to 1038) stopped the custom of long engagements (the *chuppa* was set for the first Wednesday a year after the betrothal) between the *erusin* (betrothal) and the *nissuin* (marriage) – this is where the Yiddish expression "*a yahr un a mitvoch* (a year plus a Wednesday)" comes from (*Kesubos* 2a). The sequence of today's custom, based on how it was done in Eastern Europe, involves three stages: the *vort* ("word"), *tenaim*, and finally the wedding ceremony. Because of halachic concerns, the *tenaim* is done at the same time as the wedding. Otherwise couples may need a *get* if they breach the terms of the *tenaim* and call the wedding off. The issue is this: at the *tenaim* an earthenware utensil is broken and can never be restored; likewise a finalized engagement may not be broken. The problem is that Jewish law provides strict guidelines on how to dissolve a marriage (*get*) but not how to rescind a *tenaim*. A glass goblet is broken at the end of the *chuppa*, because broken glass (unlike shattered earthenware) can be restored by melting it into a new goblet, a reminder that Jerusalem will one day be rebuilt.

there is a promise from each side not to "hide away nor conceal anything from each other."

Harmless bickering is thus normal. But remember: when talking to your spouse refrain from using harsh language.

> Leah takes her husband to a psychiatrist for a checkup. After examining him, the doctor pulls her aside and says, "It doesn't look good. I'm afraid your husband's mind has completely gone."
>
> "I'm not surprised," she replies, "he's been giving me a piece of it every day for the last thirty years!"

Hostile bickering is destructive, leaving emotional scars and the dignity of the home dangerously chipped.

The Torah says this applies especially to the husband, a warning of *onaas ishto*, "not to cause one's wife pain through one's words" – or any other body language: "the look alone," notes Moshe ibn Ezra, "explains the word!"

"A severe glance," wrote the nineteenth-century Russian-Yiddish satirist Shalom Jacob Abramovitz, aka Mendele, "may frighten more than a hundred ships!"

Yet don't hold back your emotions. It's unhealthy and is a major cause for many psychological disorders in a marriage.

So if there's gonna be smoke – make sure there's no fire, just smoked salmon!

> Cyril is driving down Madison Ave when he gets pulled over by a cop. Walking up to Cyril's car, the cop says, "I've come to tell you that your wife fell out of your car some two miles back."
>
> "Oh, *baruch Hashem* (thank God)," Cyril replies, "I thought I'd gone deaf!"

You have to get married every minute, not just on your wedding day.

To emphasize this ongoing obligation, the Torah places special emphasis on a couple's first year of marriage, because it sets the tone for the future.[35] In Judaism, one's future success depends on how one begins.[36]

The Torah exempts newlyweds (*chasanim*) from military service for the first year after their marriage. Rav Shlomo Zalman Auerbach would remind *chasanim* that the army exemption might last a year, but the end of the Torah verse ("He should bring joy to his wife...") is an independent obligation that lasts a lifetime.

The *Chazon Ish*, in his *Igeres Hakodesh*, has some advice for husbands in their *shana rishona* (first year of marriage). Before they leave the house, husbands should tell their wives where they are going. When they get back they should tell them where they've been, how it went, who they met, etc.

Was the *Chazon Ish* endorsing idle chatter? No.

He was lobbying for marital communication (one man says to another, "My wife thinks I put football before marriage, even though we just celebrated our third season together!"). He also advised a traveling husband to either phone home or write his wife a letter every day, and to bring gifts from the places he visits.

---

35. *Devarim* 24:5.
36. Rabbi Moshe Isserles (*Rema*) warns the groom not to fight with his in-laws over money, and if he does, he will be known as a "*noseh isha l'shem mammon* (one who marries for money)," and his marriage will not thrive (*Shulchan Aruch, Even Ha'ezer* 2:1). In general, Jewish courts do not get involved in family money disputes between parents and marriageable children, despite the Torah command which obligates parents to marry off their children. If they do, it's usually on behalf of the daughter where the *beis din* pressures parents to give at least a minimal support (*Chelkas Mechokek* 162; *Shulchan Aruch, Even Ha'ezer* 58). Rema writes, "Even though one is commanded to give his daughter a proper wedding gift, we do not force him in this matter; rather, whatever he wants to give, he gives" (*Shulchan Aruch, Even Ha'ezer* 70:1). Parents are also not required to go into debt to help marry off their children (*Az Nidbaru* 9:51). The Steipler, quoting Rav Yisroel Salanter, considered wealth a disadvantage for a girl because a husband could easily get used to the higher standards of living which "will cool the young man's enthusiasm for Torah study." He added that the only advantage of a rich father-in-law was that the husband could be bailed out in times of trouble (Rabbi Yaakov Yisroel Kanievsky, *Beis Rebbe*; *Kreina d'Igressa*; *Orchos Rabbeinu Baal Hakehillos Yaakov*).

In the olden days, the *chasan* was supported for the first year of marriage (*kest*) so that he could learn Torah full-time. This was based on the *Zohar*, "And these twelve months are from her [his wife] – i.e., she willingly subordinated any material benefits from her husband going out to work for the first year to his increased Torah knowledge.[37]

> Yankie and Suri have a big argument and don't talk to each other for days. Finally, on the third day, Yankie asks his wife where one of his shirts is.
>
> "Oh," she replies, "so now you're speaking to me!"
>
> Yankie looks confused. "What are you talking about?"
>
> "Haven't you noticed I haven't spoken to you for three days?!"
>
> "Actually, no," he replies, "I just thought we were getting along!"

Listening is communication without words, an act that transcends the barriers of words and language. The sound of your spouse's voice is the essence of who he or she is.

Listen to it with respect – and *shalom bayis* will appear as surely as the rabbit out of the magician's hat.

There's a reason that the center of our davening is the *Sh'ma*, which means "Hear!"[38]

Listening is thus critical to spiritual understanding. It demands great patience and discipline. Life is so busy that we often can't stop long enough to listen. Listening takes practice, but, for harmony in the home, it's well worth it.

> After the funeral, the rabbi is riding back with the deceased's son. "What were your father's last words?" the *rav* asks.
>
> "He had no last words, Rabbi. My mother was with him to the end!"

Courage, as defined by Sir Winston Churchill, "is not just to stand up and speak but also to know when to sit down and listen."

Shlomo Hamelech (King Solomon) begged God to "give me the gift of a lis-

---

37. *Zohar, Ki Seitzei.*
38. *Devarim* 6:4.

tening heart." Concerned that his followers talked impulsively without thinking, the chassidic rebbe reminded them, "We have two ears and only one mouth, in order to listen more than talk!"

So if you want *shalom bayis*, make sure your conversation is not a monologue.

As that old philosopher observed, "Tell me and I'll forget; show me and I'll remember; involve me and I'll understand!"

> Ivan is getting on in years and has serious hearing problems. He goes to the doctor who gives him a set of hearing aids and tells him he will now be able to hear 100 percent. A month later Ivan returns for a checkup and the doctor says, "Ivan! Good news! Your hearing is perfect. Your family must be relieved that you can hear again."
>
> "Oh, I haven't told them yet," he replies. "I just sit around and listen to the conversations. In fact, I've changed my will three times!"

A man goes to a psychiatrist and complains, "Nobody listens to me!" to which the doctor responds, "Next!"

To listen, says ibn Gabriel, "is to learn!" And if speaking is silver, goes the Yiddish adage, then listening is gold.

Patient eardrums ("Lend me an ear!") are the most underrated weapons in the fight for *shalom bayis*. Listening is an art. You must master it, like that wise old owl who sat on an oak: the more he saw the less he spoke; the less he spoke, the more he heard – and that's how he grew wise!

Or put in Biblical terms: Who speaks, sows; who listens, reaps!

One of the things the Jews at Sinai agreed to do was *nishma*, "we will listen." By analogy, at Sinai, Jews first promised "to do" (*asiya*) and only then "to listen," in that they would do mitzvos even if they didn't (as yet) understand why.

They were content that the knowledge would come later. Immediately after the *chuppa* ("doing"), couples need to start – and never stop – listening.

Miriam goes to her doctor and complains that her husband talks in his sleep. "Well," says the doctor, "I'll give you a mild sedative to help you sleep."

"No, no, no," she replies, "give me something to stay awake! I don't want to miss a thing!"

Shalom bayis requires paying attention. *To listen well is as essential a means of marital influence as talking well, and sometimes even more powerful.*

Remember: no one cares how much you know, until they know how much you care! So make your spouse feel worth listening to, and that what he or she says is stimulating.

People know: listening is a genuine attitude of the heart, a desire to be with another and listen to his or her thoughts, feelings and needs. In marriage each side seeks the freedom and respect to express personal feelings with full attention and no interruption.

At a White House party, a woman approached Calvin Coolidge, famed for his silence, and said "Mr. President, I made a bet I can get more than two words out of you."

He replied: "You lose."

As that saying goes: Men who know little say much; men who know much say little!

To which Henry D. Thoreau adds: "It takes two to speak the truth – one to speak and another to hear!"

The more you listen, the more your spouse will open up.

When this happens, *shalom bayis* has a window of peace to enter through. Both speaker and listener will appreciate each other more, and the duet dance of loving friendship can begin again.

Florent Schmitt, famous French composer, had a theory: *"When I don't like a piece of music – I make a point of listening to it even more closely!"* In his fund-raising speeches, Republican Speaker of the House of Representatives J. Dennis Hastert likes to tell how he visited a high school principal to see if he might want the job himself. Outside the principal's office were half a dozen chairs that were filled with problematic students in the morning and with problematic teachers during lunch hour; the job consisted of listening to complaints all day. "I couldn't see myself doing that," Hastert says. "So I decided to be a state legislator.... Right

outside my office now there are seven or eight chairs. And they're full every day."
He pauses for laughter. "They call me the Speaker, but they really ought to call
me the Listener."

Well into his old age, Groucho Marx resisted throwing in his one-liners
when in company. "I stopped because I realized I was killing conversation, and I
realized I had stopped listening!"

> Sammy and Suzie are out on vacation in the Wild West when
> they come across an Indian lying on his stomach with his ear
> to the ground. Sammy turns to his wife and says, "See that
> Indian? He's listening to the ground. He can hear things for
> miles in any direction. Just from listening!"
>
> "Wow!" she says. "Ask him what he can hear."
>
> The Indian then got up, dusted himself down, and said,
> "Covered wagon, about two miles away. Have two horses, one
> brown, one white. Man, woman, child, household effects in
> wagon."
>
> "That's incredible!" Sammy exclaims. "This Indian knows
> how far away they are, how many horses, what color they are,
> who is in the wagon, and what is in the wagon. Just from
> listening to the ground! That's amazing!"
>
> The Indian looks at him, and says, "Yep, ran over me
> about a half hour ago."

Listening is a critical part of the package of communication. The other part, of
course, is speaking! And we all know that honesty is the best policy.

Or is it? Can you tell a lie for the sake of peace?

Yes, despite the daily warning during *Shacharis* ("A person should speak the
truth within his heart..."), despite the fact that God despises liars, and despite the
transgression of the concept of *ein piv v'libo shavin* (the mouth and the heart do
not match, i.e., conveying dishonest sentiments).[39]

Our Sages agree that there are circumstances wherein the need to preserve
a respectful, stable and harmonious home trumps the integrity of absolute truth
(Yaakov was considered a man of truth, and yet he lied to Eisav and Lavan when
he had no other choice).

---

39. *Tehillim* 15; *Pesachim* 113b; *Yoma* 72b; *Yoma* 72b.

At times "truth" can be more painful than a lie, causing a mortally wounded *shalom bayis*. It can break a heart, introduce damage, pain and humiliation, and crush a spouse's spirit. In such a case, speaking the truth is totally at odds with *ahavas chesed* (love of kindness, i.e., the ideal we should strive for). Thus, it sometimes needs to take a back seat!

Remember: hurting another's feelings is also a Torah prohibition![40]

God Himself established this precedent when, in order to avoid any ill feelings, He inaccurately quoted Sarah to Avraham in respect to his old age. Sarah's response to God was an incredulous "but my husband is old!" But God tactfully tells Avraham that she said, "and I am old."[41]

The timing is important. With the pending birth of Yitzchak they are about to become a family.

At this moment, it was worth bartering truth for *shalom bayis*.

> A rich old man, who inherited all his money from his father, one day asks his young wife, "Honey, would you still have married me if my father hadn't left me with all this money?"
>
> "Of course, honey," she smiles back at him gently, "I would have married you no matter who gave you the money!"

To perfect conflict resolution, Jewish law allows bending the truth (*mutar leshanos mipnei hashalom*), known in English as "a white lie" ("white" being used in the context of "harmless"). This means being tactful and economical with the truth; telling a polite, well-intentioned, unimportant untruth to spare feelings is OK *mipnei darkei shalom*, "to maintain peace, or to save others from embarrassment."[42]

"A man may flatter his wife for the sake of marital peace," concludes *Otzar Midrashim*,[43] because nothing should be said or done in a marriage that doesn't reinforce happiness, security and peace.

Was this always the rabbinic consensus? No.

In the Talmud, the yeshivas of Hillel and Shamai couldn't agree on how to speak to a bride. Basing his decision on a Torah verse, "Distance yourself from

---

40. *Vayikra* 25:17.
41. *Bereishis* 18:12–13; *Yevamos* 65b; *Vayikra Rabba* 9:9.
42. *Yevamos* 65b; *Sanhedrin* 11a.
43. *Kesubos* 117a.

every false thing,"[44] Shamai wanted to stick to the truth no matter how painful it might be (Look! The bride is ugly...or deformed...or lame...or a midget...).

In contrast, Hillel taught that, even if the reality was not so, all brides must be called "gorgeous and extraordinary."[45]

Jewish law also suspends other laws in order to preserve harmony between husband and wife.

For example: A public vow that cannot normally be nullified is, if necessary, nullified in order to preserve harmony between spouses; and the Torah permits the holy name of God to be erased in water (in the course of the Sota ritual) in order to restore peace to the husband-wife relationship.[46]

> After a fierce quarrel, Shirley screams at her husband, "You know, I was a fool when I married you!"
>
> "Yes, dear," he calmly replies, "but I was in love – and didn't notice."

Good communication and regular dialogue, which must start *before* the *chuppa*, are the keys to *shalom bayis*. Some have it as a natural-born trait, others need to develop it. Everybody communicates, even as they need to "blow off steam"!

The question is: how?

Belittlement defeats the purpose of peace in the home; sensitivity to another view is mandatory. Don't preach, don't be impetuous or condescending (the Rambam considered preaching a form of "babbling"!).

Think before you talk. According to a Midrash, God revised the Torah *four times* before giving it to Israel![47]

Before escalating any issue to a war footing, decide how important it is to you. Good faith in marriage requires that you maintain and sustain a nonthreatening, nonconfrontational stance, acquiesce over trivialities, discuss serious disputes with patience and mutual respect.

---

44. *Shemos* 23:7.
45. *Kesubos* 16b–17a.
46. Rema, *Yoreh Deah* 228:21; *Chullin* 141a; *Nedarim* 66b.
47. Acha, *Shemos Rabba* 40:1.

> An elderly Jewish lady approaches a man at a bus stop in Brooklyn. She tugs on the sleeve of his coat and asks, "*Farshtayn Yiddish?* (Understand Yiddish?)"
>
> The man answers, "*Ya, ich farshtay* (Yes, I understand)."
>
> So the elderly lady says, "Vot time is it?"

Conversation is the exquisite glue of *shalom bayis*. Try some two-word sentences like "Thank you," "Excuse me," "I'm sorry," "You're welcome!"[48]

Keep voices low, and watch your body language. Don't let little things linger and fester. They corrode the relationship and will eventually build up and explode into a war of words way out of proportion to whatever's going on.

> The newlywed girl knocks on the door of a fortune teller. She enters a dark, hazy room, and stares into a crystal ball as the mystic delivers devastating news. "I'm sorry, there's no easy way to say this, so I'll just be blunt. I know you've only just been married a year or two but prepare yourself to be a widow. Your husband will die a violent death this year."
>
> The young wife is visibly shaken. She stares at the fortune teller's lined face, then at the single flickering candle, then down at her hands, then takes a few deep breaths to compose herself. "I need to know," she asks as she steadies her voice, "Will I be found guilty?"

Take a closer look at the Torah account of Miriam speaking *loshen hora* (degrading gossip) against her brother Moshe. God was angry but He displayed self-control, saying to her, "Listen, please, to My words."[49]

God uses the gentle, *menschlich* tone ("please"), knowing it's the most effective. It's not aggressive, it's not on the attack. And therein lies its impact.

The Rambam codifies this approach in halacha: rebuke can only be given in a soft voice, with no ill will, shame, or hurt;[50] *kal vachomer* (how much more so) with a wife!

And so the Gemora warns husbands to be careful in how they treat their

---

48. Did you hear about the dyslexic hypochondriac husband who roamed the house all day saying "*Yo Yav!*"

49. *Bamidbar* 12:6.

50. *Hilchos Deios* 6.

wives:[51] "Rabbi Helbo said, A man must be always careful with his wife's honor because blessing is found in his home only because of his wife, as the Torah says, 'And God gave good to Avraham because of her – Sara, his wife.'"[52]

Here's a useful rule of thumb: try not to use the word "you" – as in, "*You* never," "*You* don't," "*You* always," "Why can't *you*," etc.

Remember: no two people think alike. Mankind was created with differences of opinion. Men and women react differently to pressures. Women, our Sages remind us, are "more emotional [and] their tears flow more easily"; in contrast, men's egos are more easily bruised.[53]

In a letter to a husband, the Lubavitcher Rebbe urged him not to speak to his wife "with testiness and irritability (*ongetzoigenkeit*), but with kindliness and affability (*hasboras panim*)."

> Charlie says to his *chaver*, "You know, I haven't spoken to my wife for four months."
> "Really? Why not?"
> "Because I didn't want to interrupt her!"

Try not to bring religion into your dispute. You could easily box yourself into a paradox, for the reason the Torah was given in the first place, explains the Rambam at the conclusion of *Hilchos Chanuka*, is because "Great is peace!"

Therefore any contradictory quote, no matter how reputable the rabbinic or Torah source, is out of context.

"Frum" people, who have embraced higher standards in life, in particular need to behave appropriately in marriage.

There's an old Yiddish saying: after the wedding, the husband becomes a *machmir*, which means "strict, stringent" – as in, *mach mir* (make me) a cup of tea, *mach mir* something to eat, etc.

There is a rabbinic term for a learned husband with bad middos: *chamor nosei seforim*, he's nothing more than a "donkey carrying books!"

His Torah is purely academic. It has no practical application. It is a destabilizing factor in *shalom bayis*. He is a contradiction in his own Torah terms.

---

51. *Bava Metzia* 58, 59.
52. *Bereishis* 12:16.
53. *Shabbas* 33b; *Kiddushin* 80b; *Bava Metzia* 59a; *Brachos* 32b, 58a.

Commandments of the Torah, warns Rabbeinu Yona, can only be fulfilled in a peaceful atmosphere.

The fact is this: Shabbas-observant or not, at the first sight and sound of discord, the *Shechina* disappears.

With the first hint of serious familial *machlokes*, your household is at risk. How to respond? Here's Rabban Shimon Ben Gamliel's solution: "*Kol yomai gadalti bein hachachamim v'lo matzasi laguf tov ela shtika* (All my days I have grown up among the Sages and I have not found anything better for the body than silence)." The best way to stop a disagreement from escalating is…silence!

"Keep calm, and be quiet," advises Yeshayahu.[54]

The Gemora is more blunt: "Muzzle your mouth at the time of a quarrel!"[55]

In other words, let your ego take a holiday. Keeping quiet ("A soft reply will turn away anger")[56] is not an admission of being wrong. It's a sign of maturity and *seichel*!

> The phone rings in the *rav's* study late one night. "Yes, who is it?" he asks.
>
> "Oh, Rabbi," says the voice on the other end of the line, crying hysterically, "This is Esther, your neighbor. I'm so sorry to bother you so late at night, but I've got terrible news."
>
> "What happened, Esther?"
>
> "Oy! My husband passed away late last night, Rabbi."
>
> "Oh, no, Esther. *Baruch dayan ha'emes*, blessed is the True Judge. That's terrible. You must be in shock. Tell me, Esther, did he have any last requests?"
>
> "Well, actually, he did have one, Rabbi."
>
> "What was it?"
>
> "He said, 'Please, please, Esther, have *rachmanus*! Put down the gun…'"

---

54.   *Yeshayahu* 7:4.
55.   *Chullin* 89a.
56.   *Mishlei* 15:1.

Rav Shimshon Raphael Hirsch on the Marital *Shechina*

Rav Shimshon Raphael Hirsch writes that the *kohen gadol* (high priest) embodies the moral ideal of the entire Jewish people. His is supposed to provide a role model to which every Jew can aspire – a model of moral excellence and completion. The foundation of this development and completion is marriage – the state that Chazal said is also the basis of all true happiness. This is why the *kohen gadol* may only perform the *avoda* of Yom Kippur while married. Having once been married is not enough; to do the *avoda*, the *kohen gadol* had to be living within the state of marriage.

The Ramak (Rabbi Moshe Cordovero) explains the depths of this law. Until one marries, it is obvious that the *Shechina* is absent from a man's life, because the *Shechina* only rests upon a man in the merit of his wife. So if a man does not get along with his wife, it is clear that the *Shechina* is not "living in harmony" with him either! It is important to realize how indebted we are to our spouses, and must work hard to ensure that they do not harbor any resentments against us. It is all too easy to take one's wife for granted, forgetting that "A woman of valor is her husband's crown."[57]

---

57. *Mishlei* 12:4.

The Test of the Three Truths

In ancient Greece (469–399 BCE), Socrates was widely lauded for his wisdom. One day the great philosopher came upon an acquaintance, who ran up to him excitedly and said, "Socrates, do you know what I just heard about one of your students?"

"Wait a moment," Socrates replied. "Before you tell me, I'd like you to pass a little test. It's called the Test of Three."

"Test of Three?"

"That's correct," Socrates continued. "Before you talk to me about my student let's take a moment to test what you're going to say. The first test is Truth. Have you made absolutely sure that what you are about to tell me is true?"

"No," the man replied, "actually I just heard about it."

"All right," said Socrates. "So you don't really know if it's true or not. Now let's try the second test, the test of Goodness. Is what you are about to tell me about my student something good?"

"No, on the contrary..."

"So," Socrates continued, "you want to tell me something bad about him even though you're not certain it's true?"

The man shrugged, a little embarrassed.

Socrates continued, "You may still pass though because there is a third test – the filter of Usefulness. Is what you want to tell me about my student going to be useful to me?"

"No, not really..."

"Well," concluded Socrates, "if what you want to tell me is neither True nor Good nor even Useful, why tell it to me at all?"

The man felt ashamed – and said no more.

Rav Yaakov Kamenetsky Talks to His *Rebbetzin*

Rav Yaakov Kamenetsky was engrossed in a conversation at a wedding when he realized that his wife was trying to catch his attention. Rav Yaakov quickly approached his wife and asked, "What is it that the *Rebbetzin* wants?"

"I wanted to know when the *Rav* wants to leave," she responded.

"Whenever the *Rebbetzin* wants to go," was his quick response.

"I'd like to go whenever the *Rav* wants to leave," she answered.

"The Gemora states that 'heavenly matters' are decided by the husband and 'worldly matters' by the wife. It seems to me that this is a 'worldly matter,'" Rav Yaakov replied.

"For me, listening to the *Rav* is a 'heavenly matter,'" his wife countered.

"Well, in that case, my 'heavenly matter' decision is that we should go when you want!" Rav Yaakov persisted.

"Well, in that case, I'd like to remain another thirty minutes," concluded his wife.

Rav Yaakov smiled and said, "We'll remain another thirty minutes."

Rav Shmuel Aron Yudelevitz on Conflict

A man once went to Rav Shmuel Aron Yudelevitz and told him about a husband and wife who disagreed about using public electricity in Israel on Shabbas. The husband did not want to use the electricity provided by the electric company because of the problems of *chillul Shabbas* that were involved. His wife, on the other hand, was used to eating her Shabbas meals in bright light and was upset at the notion of having to eat in the dim light of a single lantern. This led to bitter arguments. She claimed that she had no *oneg Shabbas* while having to manage with a single light while he argued back that halacha forbids the use of electricity provided by a Jew on Shabbas. The man asked Rav Shmuel Aron Yudelevitz for advice on how to resolve this issue.

"There is no question that there is good reason not to use electricity on Shabbas," said Rav Shmuel Aron. "However, the husband must not forget that Hashem allowed His holy name to be erased in order to bring peace between husband and wife, so there is certainly basis to follow the more lenient opinion in this matter as well. What good is there in avoiding the use of electricity on Shabbas if it will spark the fire of conflict? The Torah tells us 'not to ignite a fire in any of your dwellings on the Shabbas day,' whether it is in the form of fire, electricity or conflict!"

The Talmud Debates Peace in the Home

Rav said, "A man must always be careful not to cause pain to his wife. Because she cries easily she is quickly hurt.'"

Said Rabbi Elazar, "When the *Beis HaMikdash* was destroyed, the gates of prayer were shut, but the gates of tears are not shut."[58]

Rav also said, "A man who follows his wife's advice will descend into Gehinnom."

Rabbi Papa argued with Abaye..., "People say that if your wife is short, bend down and listen to her whisper." It is no contradiction: the one [following your wife's advice will send you straight to the netherworld] refers to religious matters, and the other [listening to your wife's whispered counsel] refers to household matters."

Rabbi Hisda said, "All the heavenly gates [of prayer] are shut except the gates of *onaa* (hurt feelings)."

Rabbi Elazar said, "All punishments come by means of a messenger except for punishment for *onaa*." [God reserves punishment for *onaa* to be meted out directly by Himself.][59]

Rabbi Helbo said, "A man must always honor his wife, because blessings come to a man's home only on her account."

– Bava Metzia 59a

---

58. This does not mean that a person can't communicate with God in prayer, but rather that the prayers are not automatically heard without some further effort.

59. There are only two other sins that God punished directly: robbery and idolatry.

Rav Avrohom Pam
on Communication

Being considerate of one's wife calls for vigilance, especially in areas of speech. We tend to be careless with what we say, and yet a harsh word can inflict wounds that never heal. In general human relationships, the Torah prohibits *onas devarim*, "causing pain with words," on which the *Sefer Hachinuch* elaborates, "One must not say anything that will pain or anguish someone, and leave him helpless." Now if this is the case in regard to strangers, imagine how much more sensitive the Torah expects one to be towards his wife. A harsh word, a demeaning expression, an insulting remark, any of these can severely strain a marriage. A derogatory name hurled out in anger can inflict a wound that continues to fester long after the reasons for the argument are forgotten....

When two lives become so intertwined and mutually dependent as do the lives of a husband and wife, then their relationship is so sensitive that a word or expression uttered in innocence can cause deep hurt and actually threaten *shalom bayis*."

– Rav Avrohom Pam, *zt"l, rosh yeshiva* Mesivta Torah Vodaas

The Ponovezher Rav on Keeping a House Tidy

A resident of the town of Ponovezh once went to the Ponovezher Rav, Rabbi Yosef Shlomo Kahanamen, requesting that the *rav* arrange a *get* for him. The *rav* asked him why he wanted to divorce his wife, and he explained that her untidiness was getting on his nerves to the point where he could stand it no longer. Disturbed by this answer, the *rav* told him that this was not grounds for divorce and sent him home. However, the man kept on coming back, and the *rav* soon realized that he would not give up. With no other option, the *rav* said to him, "Meet me tomorrow morning at my home."

In the meantime, the *rav* asked his *rebbetzin* to turn over the entire house and create an appalling mess. When the man arrived the next day, he was in shock. With very few words the *rav* said to him, "You would probably say that I, too, should divorce my wife." The man thought about it for a few minutes and then had a change of heart.

As they say, it's better to give than to *get*!

Tip 1:
Comedy

Tip 2:
Communication, Conversation

Tip 3: Common Sense

Tip 4:
Compromise, Causation

Tip 5:
Caring, Compassion, Courtesy

Tip 6:
Commonality, Compatibility, Commitment

Tip 7:
Camaraderie, Companionship

Too many folks prepare for a wedding,
but not for a marriage!

One day the newlywed calls her mother in tears, crying, "Moishie doesn't appreciate what I do for him."

"Now, now," her mother comforts her, "I'm sure it's just a misunderstanding. Tell me what happened."

"Well, I bought a frozen turkey roll and he yelled and screamed at me about the price!"

"That's not right," her mother replies. "Those turkey rolls are only a few dollars!"

"No, mama. It wasn't the price of the turkey, it's the airplane ticket."

"Airplane ticket? Why did you need an airplane ticket?"

"Well, Mama, when I got home I read the directions on the package and it said, 'Prepare from a frozen state' – so I flew to Alaska!"

Common Sense Is Not So Common!

> Beryl and his wife Sheindy are driving home late one night after a Purim party and get pulled over by the police. "Your tail light is burned out," the officer explains.
>
> "I'm sorry, officer, I didn't realize it was out, I'll get it fixed right away."
>
> "I knew this would happen," Sheindy yells, "I told you two days ago to get that light fixed!"
>
> The officer then looks at Beryl's license and says, "Sir, your license has expired."
>
> "I'm sorry, officer, I didn't realize it had expired, I'll take care of it first thing in the morning."
>
> "I told you over a week ago," Sheindy yells again, "that the state sent you a letter telling you that your license had expired!"
>
> Beryl, upset at his wife for interjecting, starts screaming at her to shut up. The police officer leans through the window and says, "Ma'am, does your husband always talk to you like that?"
>
> "Oh, no, officer," she replies, "only when he's drunk!"

A sign posted on a refrigerator read: "Be careful of the words you say. Keep them soft and sweet. You'll never know from day to day, which ones you'll have to eat!"

Take your choice: nonsense or common sense!

Having common sense (in Hebrew, *seichel hayashar*, "straight thinking"), helps you navigate your way through life. *Seichel tov*, "good common sense," is just another way of saying "paying attention to the obvious."

Marriage and maturity are not necessarily mutual terms. No relationship can survive irrationality, nor the lack of good judgment, nor stupid advice ("I came home and found my wife bent over cooking on a hot stove so I immediately rushed out and got her a taller stove!").

Hob seichel! Zei nisht kein nahr! was a common refrain in *cheder* when I was growing up. It means, "Have some common sense! Don't be a fool!"

To be considered a fool was the most humiliating of all charges.

Albert Einstein would confide in his diary that "Nothing astonishes people so much as those with common sense!" Or as Victor Hugo, nineteenth-century French novelist, statesman, and human rights campaigner put it: "Common sense is in spite of, not the result of, education."

"Two things are infinite," concluded Albert Einstein, "the universe and human stupidity; and I'm not so sure about the universe!"

And one of life's greatest mysteries is how the boy who wasn't good enough to marry your daughter can be the father of the smartest grandchild in the world!

> *Nebach*, poor Yankie had finally gone mad from all the shouting and fighting in his house. His wife took him to a psychiatrist, who suggested he might have to go to a psych ward. "How do you decide whether to institutionalize a patient?" she asks.
>
> "Well," the doctor replies, "we fill a bathtub, then offer a teaspoon, a teacup and a bucket to the patient, and ask him to empty the tub."
>
> "I get it," she interrupts. "A normal person would use the bucket because it's the biggest."
>
> "No," the psychiatrist replies. "A normal person would just pull the plug!"

A favorite short saying of Rav Yaakov Kamenetsky was: "*Man darf zein normal* (a person ought to be normal)."

Many marriages buckle under the weight of plain stupidity, a paralyzing disadvantage to a normal, peaceful household. An ounce of down-to-earth wisdom (*chochma*) goes a long way towards *shalom bayis*; and, if you're fortunate to have it, goes *Mishlei*, then "all your paths are peace!"[1]

---

1. *Mishlei* 3:13.

The wise men of Chelm once got together to solve the problem of life. They decided one of the main problems of life is that everyone has worries. If people didn't have any worries, then life would be easy. But how to stop folks from worrying?

Why not hire somebody to do all the worrying so everyone else could have it easy? The idea was brilliant. Yes, it would be tough job, but they would pay the man well to make up for it. So everybody in the town chipped in fifty rubles a month to hire someone to do all the town's worrying for them.

This went on for a while, until the rabbi, the wisest of them all, started thinking. "If the man is making fifty rubles a month, what has he got to worry about?"[2]

Rav Chaim Leib Shmuelevitz, *rosh yeshiva* of Mir, noticed that when folks get involved in disputes, they lose their common sense (or "lose their cool"). Adds Rav Yissocher Frand: "There is an overriding tendency to throw away one's common sense and jump into the blinding dynamics of *machlokes*. Maintaining common sense in moments of tension requires great wisdom."

In his sefer *Malmad Hatalmidim*, twelfth-century French rabbi Yaakov Anatoli calls wisdom "the soul's natural food." But, warns eleventh-century Spanish moralist Bachya ben Yosef ibn Pakuda in his *sefer Chovos Halevavos*, if you misuse *seichel* in your relationship "it becomes an incurable disease!"

Freddie's walking down the street with his two new dogs when he bumps into his *chaver* who asks what their names are.

"Well, this one's called Rolex."

"Rolex? What's the other dog called?"

"Timex."

"Wow! Those are weird names for dogs."

"Not at all! They're watch dogs!"

---

2. A Chelmite scientist wanted to know where the sun went after it set. He went around asking the other scientists, but they didn't know either. Pretty soon he had the whole department trying to figure it out. They puzzled over it for a long time but they couldn't come up with an answer. In fact they sat up all night thinking about it. Finally it dawned on them!

A *vort* from Rabbi Chaim Pinchas Scheinberg:

> Our emotions always challenge our intellect. Life is a clash
> between the *seichel* and the *nefesh,* which is the interaction
> between our *yetzer hatov* and our *yetzer hora.* The *seichel* is
> our God-given ability to reason. The *sefer Chovos Halevavos*
> uses the specific phrases "*omar haseichel*" and "*omar hanef-
> esh*" to describe this constant dialogue between intellect and
> emotion.[3] The home is a place where we think we can be
> "ourselves." Nothing can be further from the truth. At home,
> we have to be better than ourselves. We are angered much
> more easily at home. We lose control. We say and do many
> things that are not nice. We cause people pain. We become a
> source of suffering rather than a source of joy. At home, our
> defenses are down. We have no public image to protect. We
> view the home as a refuge from the pressures of the outside
> world. At home, we are often tired and hungry. We seek the
> comforts of home; consequently, we do not look forward to
> its challenges, nor are we always ready to cope with its pres-
> sures. We flare up if something is not to our liking.
>
> The *seichel* cannot function while we are angry. Our
> emotions overwhelm our sense of reason. They paralyze our
> ability to estimate the damage that our words and actions
> can cause. Taking vengeance for our own frustrations and
> disappointments becomes more important than concern for
> the feelings of our beloved ones. Emotions and *seichel* cannot
> operate at the same time. If we lack education and training
> about how to manage our emotions, then this battle rages
> throughout life. The *seichel* is a great commander. However
> if, through lack of proper training, we do not heed the *seichel,*
> then the *seichel* is powerless. Therefore, people who are
> concerned and aware of these dangers train themselves to
> be able to heed the voice of their *seichel.* They learn to give
> preference to the *seichel's* commands rather than their emo-
> tional needs. Such individuals achieve *menuchas hanefesh.*

---

3.   *Shaar Avodas Elokim* 5.

They have *shalom*. They are at peace with themselves. They
are at peace with their spouses and their children. They are
at peace with their neighbors and they are at peace with the
world. We cannot ignore our emotions, but we can direct
them. The emotions can become submissive to the *seichel*.
Then they will be manageable instead of assertive.

The *yeshiva bochur* arrives at his rebbe's study to take his *smicha* test. The first
question is, "Name the five volumes of the *Shulchan Aruch*."

The student, thinking that his rebbe made an innocent mistake, names the
four volumes (*Orach Chayim, Yore Deah, Even Ha'ezer, Choshen Mishpat*) but,
again, the rebbe persists and asks him to name the fifth.

"There is no fifth volume," the boy answers.

"You are mistaken" his rebbe replies. "Common sense is the fifth volume, and
if you don't have it, all your rulings will be of no use, even if you know the other
four volumes by heart!"

"I wish I'd brought our piano with us," the husband says to his
wife as they stand in line at the airport ticket counter.
"Why?" she asks.
"Because our passports are on it!"

The Midrash credits *seichel* as the main factor for the success of the daughters of
Tzelafchad in negotiations with Moshe over a share of the Holy Land.[4]

By singling out their common sense (in their timing to present their argument) as the mother of all virtues, the Midrash lays the foundation for the "fifth
Shulchan Aruch"; one can possess intellectual knowledge, great talent and brilliant
abilities but absent *seichel*, one will still fail in life.

Far better, teaches the "fifth Shulchan Aruch," to have a dose of *seichel* without
the knowledge – than much knowledge without the *seichel*!

Brian and Bernie buy a racehorse together and are searching
for a name. "Let's call him Swift Feet," says Brian.
"Swift Feet? That's a stupid name."
"You have a better suggestion?"
"Yeah. Let's call him Bad News."

---

4. *Bamidbar Rabba* 21:10.

"Bad News? Why Bad News?"

"Because everybody knows that bad news travels fast!"

Rabbi Avrohom Blumenkrantz, an expert in marital counseling, once told me about a couple who fought on the first morning after the wedding. He wanted a glass of orange juice and she told him to get it from the fridge. He replied that his mother always gave him a glass of orange juice every morning when he woke up. She replied, "I'm not your mother!"

This led to a fight which brought them to Rav Blumenkrantz.

Neither side would budge, so he told them to go back to their parents' homes. He then called the mother of the *chasan* and told her to wean her son of orange juice. And she did. The morning juice became once every two days, then every four days, etc., until her son was off the morning habit and went back to his wife.

The moral? No *seichel*!

> Abe calls his best friend on the phone. "Hey, David, it's my parents' golden wedding anniversary next week and I want you and your wife to come to the party."
>
> "Sure, Abe," he replies, "we'll be there."
>
> "Oh," adds Abe, "don't forget to bring something gold!"
>
> So David and his wife show up with a goldfish, a jar of Gold Blend coffee and Nat Goldstein.

One sliver of *seichel*, when dipped in forbearance, can do wonders.

Rabbi Yaakov Kamentsky was once asked what his *minhag* (custom) was when it came to parents walking down the aisle to their children's *chuppa*. He replied, "My *minhag* is to do whatever the *mechutanim* (in-laws) want! Avoiding *machlokes* is the best *segula* for a happy life."

Not each fight needs to be fought, not each argument needs to be won. In fact, it's possible to get your way and still let your spouse feel like the victor. That requires *seichel*, maturity and patience.

Remember: far better to change yourself before you try to change your spouse. Stir that with a dish of midrashic advice ("End everything you do on a good note"), and you've gained several brownie points in *seichel*.

There is an insightful Gemora that talks about a jar with one pebble. If shaken, it makes a big noise.[5] But if the jar is *full* of pebbles and shaken, it makes no noise.

The analogy to *shalom bayis* is clear.

A person who makes all the noise during a dispute is essentially as empty as that pebble shaken in a jug. It signals a lack of *seichel* when couples don't speak to each other softly, and as quiet as if the jar was full, no matter how much either one is being "shaken."

> A wife was screaming at her husband after he had done something really stupid.
>
> "You know," she screams, "you're an idiot. You've always been an idiot. You'll always be an idiot. If they had an idiot contest, you'd come in second!"
>
> "Second?" he asks. "Why only second?"
>
> "Because you're an idiot!"

Unfortunately, common sense is not that common. As they say, the problem with the gene pool is that there is no lifeguard!

When spouses lack sense, it's like an invisible wall that exists between the two. That's a recipe for constant chaos, disorder and disaster – in short: marital madness that requires common sense pills to be taken daily. Remember: the Rambam traces much of the problems in life to people's own actions![6] In other words: have a *bissel seichel*!

A newlywed once complained to the Steipler Rav that his house was always a chaotic mess before Shabbas, to which the Steipler replied, "*Nu! Nemt a baizim!* (So, take a broom!)"

The ability to see the larger picture is critical to a stable marriage.

In the face of all the life decisions that each family inevitably faces, one must not get sidetracked by *narishkeit*. A person who has disciplined himself with the clarity of common sense to see the issues through does not allow his skewed perspective to turn everything into an immediate crisis.

There were once two *rabbonim* in the same town. One always seemed to be sick, catching every illness going around. The other rabbi was always fit and fine. One day he was asked, "How come that other rabbi takes every problem so

---

5.   *Bava Metzia* 85b.
6.   Rambam, *Moreh Nevuchim* 3:12.

much to heart that he gets sick himself, while you hear the same problems but are fine?"

"Well," the *rav* replied, "I learned that the best way to handle problems is to be like a duck. Everything slips off its back!"

> The *shochet* at the local butcher thought the new *chasan* in town wasn't too bright. When he came in to buy a chicken, the butcher put his last chicken on the scale, weighed it, and said, "That'll be $8.35."
>
> "I think it's a bit small. Do you have anything larger?"
>
> "Sure," says the butcher as he pretends to put the chicken in the refrigerator, pauses, then takes it out again. "This one," he says, "is $8.99."
>
> "OK. You know what, I'll take both of them!"

A woman once came to Rav Gershon Tanchum of Minsk demanding a *get*. He told her to come back in thirty days, and during that time she should go to the poor part of town and give out bread to the Jewish paupers. She never came back for the *get*. As soon as she compared her situation to that of real misery, she realized she didn't have it so bad.

Reality is like a flu shot. It may give you a quick, sharp discomfort, but it keeps your relationship healthier over the long term. Remember: every cloud has its silver lining, or in yeshivish-speak, "Every *maala* has its *chesron*!"

Seichel allows you to see reality, avoid the making-a-mountain-out-of-a-molehill syndrome, and respond with plain intelligence. You know what they say: a good marriage is ten percent *seichel* and ninety percent *mazel*, but you need a hundred percent *seichel* to develop the *mazel*!

> After his daughter comes home from her date, her father asks her, "Tell me, does this boy have any money?"
>
> "Oh, Tatte!" she replies, shaking her head sadly, "you men are all alike! That's exactly what he asked me about you!"

Those with *seichel* understand the lowest common denominator of *shalom bayis*: conflicts are resolved calmly; differences are discussed in decency and respect. *Seichel* lets you bury the hatchet quickly, gives you the ability to see the larger picture, and avoids little frictions transforming into monumental ones.

There's no reason to turn the inevitable bumps in your marriage into mountains.

For when *seichel* leaves, marital (and perhaps martial) turbulence enters.

It usually comes in the form of panic (quick, the sky is falling!). But remember: when approached with *seichel*, adversity can cement relationships.

So develop your instincts to respond maturely to issues. A quiver full of patience gives you the arrows to shoot down stupidity.

Take your time. "A nod to the wise is sufficient," sighs the wise Ben Sira, "but the fool requires a blow!"

A king once said to his favorite counselor, "Ask what you will and I shall grant it." The counselor asked for the king's daughter in marriage, knowing that all else would then be one day his; but when God asked Shlomo Hamelech what he would have, he asked for…wisdom![7]

> All eyes are on the Rebbe at his *Shabbas tisch* when suddenly an angel appears and says to him, "In return for your unselfish behavior and exemplary piety, God wants to reward you. You may choose: wisdom or wealth!"
>
> Without hesitating, the Rebbe selects wisdom.
>
> "Done!" says the angel, and disappears in a cloud of smoke and a bolt of lightning.
>
> The room is silent. All heads are turned toward the Rebbe, waiting for his first words of infinite wisdom. After several minutes of silence, the *shammas* leans over and whispers in the Rebbe's ear, "*Nu!* Say something wise!"
>
> The Rebbe lets out a deep sigh and says, "I should have taken the money!"

Common sense is the ability to instinctively size up a situation realistically – and then do and say the right thing (but remember, "well done" is always better than "well said!").

The art of conversation is not only to say the right thing in the right place, but also to leave unsaid the wrong thing at the wrong moment.

Once, during the Passover Seder, one of Rabbi Akiva Eiger's guests accidentally spilled some wine on the tablecloth. Perceiving his guest's embarrass-

---

7.   I *Melachim* 3:5; Shimon ben Chalafta, *Koheles Rabba* 1:1.

ment, Rav Eiger, displaying a combination of quick thinking and common sense, discreetly shook the table so that his cup of wine also tumbled over, then turned to his guest and said, "It seems that something's wrong with the table. It's not standing properly."

The rabbis of the Talmud ask "Who is wise?" and then answer, "those who forsee results."[8]

The I-can't-think-clearly-because-I'm-too-busy-reacting syndrome is very common. But the ability to think clearly and respond rationally are the flip sides to the *shalom bayis* coin. They go hand in hand. They are spiritual twins, joined at the hip of marriage.

To some spouses it comes naturally, to others its MIA (missing in action). But if you don't have it, get it! How? The first step is to know you need it.

> Expecting wisdom from the Far East, Beryl opens a fortune
> cookie after a meal in a Chinese restaurant and unfolds the
> message, which says, "Ignore previous cookie!"

Look in the *siddur*. The very first petition to God in the *Shemoneh Esrei* prayer, said thrice daily, is for plain intelligence, aka *seichel* (the word *intelligence* is derived from the Latin verb *intellegere*, which means "to understand"; this is a "street smart" capacity – i.e., *seichel* – which is not the same as being "book smart").[9]

First we thank God for introducing us to knowledge (*deiah*), then for the ability to understand this knowledge (*bina*), and finally, and most importantly, in a recognition that knowledge and understanding are insufficient, we ask for *haskel*, "insight," derived from the Hebrew root, *seichel*, "common sense."

> After many years studying in Israel, the large *kollel* family
> decides to return to the States. As they are packing their bags,
> the five-year-old starts saying her prayers: "God, please take
> care of our family. Also, You probably won't be hearing from
> me anymore. We're moving to New York."

---

8.   *Taanis* 32a.

9.   Rav Yitzchak Hutner once boarded a bus and saw one of his *talmidim* sitting with a *sefer*, learning on the bus. Rav Hutner turned to the *talmid* and said, "*Nu*, so when do you have time to think?"

Common sense can be developed with patience ("[Even] the *tzadik* falls seven times and gets up!"),[10] experience, maturity, or simply aging.

Remember: the word *sage* must have *age* in it!

When the Torah sets out to describe Avraham's search for a *shidduch* for his son Yitzchak, it begins the *parsha* (*Chayei Sarah*) with the words "and Avraham was *zakein* (old) well on into his years"; however, according to the Gemora there was no such thing as old age at the time of Avraham (in fact, it was sometimes difficult to tell the difference between father and son).

Avraham's "oldness" was not measured in years but in spiritual *seichel* and maturity.

Zakein is thus an acronym for *zeh shekana chochma*, "this one, who has acquired wisdom." In other words, to seek a *shidduch* requires the *seichel* that comes with age.

> Several guys are in the *mikva* area when a cell phone suddenly rings from a locker. Yossi answers it, "Yes?"
>
> "Listen, it's me," a woman says, "are you still at the *mikva*?"
>
> "Yes."
>
> "Great! I'm at the mall and I found this beautiful leather coat. It's a thousand dollars. Can I go ahead and buy it?"
>
> "Sure, why not?"
>
> "Oh, and I also stopped by the Jaguar dealership and saw the new 2009 models. They're really nice. Can I have one?"
>
> "How much is it?"
>
> "Ninety thousand dollars."
>
> "No problem!"
>
> "Oh, one more thing. Remember the house on the corner? It's back on the market. A steal at $1,750,000."
>
> "Go ahead. If you like it, it's yours!"
>
> "Oh, thank you, thank you. I'll see you later for dinner. I love you so much!"
>
> Yossi hangs up, then turns to the room and says, "Hey! Anybody know whose phone this is?"

---

10. *Mishlei* 24:16.

Seichel is another word for marital diplomacy, a word that stems from the Greek *diploma*, which literally means "folded in two." In ancient Greece, a diploma was simply a certificate, typically folded in half, certifying completion of a course.

Later, the French called their foreign legations *diplomatique,* which led to the English word *diplomacy*, which describes nonconfrontational, polite dealings with others.

Like foreign relations, human relations also have bumps in the road.

In the context of marriage, when you feel the bump, or see it coming, each side must strive for buckets full of *seichel*, a dose of tact, and the ability to reason, solve problems and think clearly.

The spouse with no *seichel* is one who has learned nothing from life's experiences, and thus cannot make sense of issues and is at a loss to figure out what to do.

Those blessed with common sense are aware: *seichel* is a stimulus for further *seichel*, or put the other way, *narishkeit* breeds *narishkeit*! Or, as that wise ol' psychologist put it, "Only two complete halves can make a complete whole!"

> Suzy brings her date home to meet her parents. When he arrives they are shocked by his rough appearance: leather jacket, motorcycle boots, tattoos, pierced nose. The anxious parents pull their daughter aside and grapple for the right words to express their concern. "Honey," says her mother, diplomatically, "he doesn't seem very...nice."
>
> "What! That's impossible," she replies, shocked. "If he weren't nice, why would he be doing five hundred hours of community service?"

"One must use his common sense," writes Rav Herschel Shachter, "and only apply the *halacha* when it makes sense.... Every exaggeration is by definition not true. It does not correspond to reality.... The challenge of *lernin* is to be able to formulate the *halacha* precisely, without any exaggeration leaning in either direction, with *seichel*."

Pirkei Avos gives us a list of seven ways to develop common sense: don't speak before your superior, don't interrupt others, don't be too quick to respond, ask and answer questions directly, be clear and articulate ("talk about first things first and last things last!"), don't be scared to admit you don't know and, finally, acknowledge the truth.[11]

Since Sages are the ones with the wisdom (the *daas* in *daas Torah* means *seichel* and knowledge), *Pirkei Avos* urges husbands and wives to turn their homes into "a meeting place" for Torah scholars – in the hope that not just their Torah knowledge but some of their *seichel* will also rub off![12]

Far better, goes that old Yiddish saying, to get a slap from a wise man than a kiss from one lacking in *seichel*!

> Sarah and her husband are sitting quietly in the den reading. Suddenly, Sarah bursts out laughing, "Listen to this. There's a classified ad here where a guy is offering to swap his wife for a season ticket to the stadium." Turning to her husband, who's engrossed in his newspaper, Sarah teases, "Say, would you swap me for a season ticket?"
> "Absolutely not," he replies.
> "Oh, that's so sweet of you. Tell me, why not?"
> "'Cause the season's more than half over!"

Some Torah linguists link the term *seichel*, as in "intellect" or "reasoning," to the word *l'haskil*, which refers to the Tree of Knowledge: "The woman saw that the tree was good for food, appealing to the eyes, and an attractive means for gaining understanding (*l'haskil*)."[13]

Rashi also sees it as a play on the word *sikel*, which means "to switch around," used in Yaakov's blessing to his two grandsons (Ephraim and Menashe).[14]

Chabad *chassidus* links the letter *shin* on each side of the head *tefillin* to the idea of *seichel*, with the three strands representing *chochma, bina,* and *daas*.[15]

The first-century Egyptian Torah philosopher Philo urged Jews to use *seichel* to "cleanse" their minds.

In his *Sefer Sha'ashuim*, Yosef Zabara, the thirteenth-century Torah physician and satirist poet from Barcelona, chose common sense as "the best pedigree" in any

---

11.   *Pirkei Avos* 5:7.
12.   *Pirkei Avos* 1:4.
13.   *Bereishis* 3:6.
14.   *Bereishis* 48:14.
15.   The word *Chabad*, incidentally, is an acronym for *chochma, bina,* and *daas*.

loving relationship, and in his commentary on *Koheles*, the twelfth-century Spanish Torah poet Avraham ibn Ezra reminds us that wisdom "begets humility."

Pondering the quality of life, Avraham's relative Moshe ibn Ezra, the twelfth-century Spanish Torah philosopher, concludes that "a short life with much common sense is better than a long life with little wisdom!"

> Yossi, the chicken farmer, was carrying a bag through the shtetl when he bumped into Moishie, his *chaver*.
>
> Moishie: "Hey, Yossi, what you got in that bag?"
>
> Yossi: "In this bag here I got me my chickens."
>
> Moishie: "Chickens! I sure could use some chickens. Say, I bet ya I can guess how many chickens you got in that that bag! And if I'm right, you'll give me one!"
>
> Yossi: "OK. If you guess how many chickens I got in this bag I'll give you both of them."
>
> Moishie: "Uhhh...five!"
>
> Yossi: "Wrong!"

Rav Avrohom Pam on *Shalom Bayis*

Since it is impossible for two people living together to agree on absolutely every-thing, it would be wise to anticipate the inevitable differences that are bound to arise. Is there any preferred way to iron out these differences so as not to strain their relationship? A recently married young man sought my advice regarding a problem that had arisen in his marriage – a problem that to me seemed to be very insignificant. When I asked him why he thought it necessary to make an issue over such an unimportant thing, he replied, "That's not the idea. Sure, I can give in on this matter. But I'm afraid that if I do, she'll dominate our marriage."

I explained to him that his basic premise was foolish. Any relationship is a two-way street. If he would yield on this issue, he would build up credit with his wife, and she, in turn, would be more than willing to please him on other issues that may be far more important to him. And it is not a matter of keeping score on major points but of dividing areas of responsibility and yielding whenever it is a matter outside of the individual's purview.

– Rav Avrohom Pam, zt"l, rosh yeshiva Mesivta Torah Vodaas

Goats and Chickens and Harmony in the Home

It happened that a poor man became so distressed, both because of how small his home was and how crowded it was, that he went to see his rebbe.

"Rebbe, I have so many children and relatives living with me, my wife and I cannot breathe in our own home."

The rabbi listened and then asked the man, "Do you have a goat?"

"A goat?" asked the man incredulously. "Why does the Rebbe ask me this question? Of course I have a goat."

"Good," said the rabbi. "My advice to you is to move the goat into your house and visit me again next week."

The man did as he was told even though the situation at home went from bad to intolerable. A week later he was at the rabbi's door.

"How is it now?" asked the rabbi.

"Impossible," said the man.

"Let me ask you a question. Do you by any chance have any chickens?" asked the rabbi, scratching his beard.

"Yes," said the man, throwing up his hands, "I have chickens."

"Good," said the rabbi, smiling. "My advice to you is to also move the chickens into your house, and come back to see me in a week."

The man could barely wait the week to return. He stood there, banging on the rabbi's door.

"So, now, how is it?" asked the rabbi.

"Impossible, simply impossible," said the man. "I cannot go on like this."

The rabbi smiled. "My advice to you is to go home and to take the chickens and the goat out of your house and come back to see me next week."

"Yes, Rebbe," said the man, anxious now to leave and do as he was told.

Next week the man stood at the rabbi's door with a broad grin and a well-rested manner.

"So how was it this past week?" asked the rabbi.

"A blessing on the Rebbe. Only the Rebbe could have solved this. My life is so much better. I don't know how to express my thanks."

Seichel in the Pits!

A group of citizens in the town of Chelm were busily engaged in digging a foundation for the new shul, when a disturbing thought occurred to one of the laborers.

"What are we going to do with all this earth we're digging up?" he asked. "We certainly can't just leave it here where our house of worship will be built."

There was a hubbub of excitement as the men rested on their spades and pondered the question. Suggestions were made and just as quickly rejected.

Suddenly one of the Chelmites smiled and held his hand up for silence. "I have the solution," he proclaimed. "We will make a deep pit, and into it we'll shovel all this earth we're digging up for the synagogue!"

A round of applause greeted this proposal, until another Chelmite raised his voice in protest. "That won't work at all! What will we do with the earth from the pit?"

There was a stunned silence as the men tried to cope with this new problem, but the first Chelmite soon provided the answer.

"It is all very simple," he said. "We'll dig another pit, and into that one we'll shovel all the earth we're digging now, and all the earth we take out of the first pit. The only thing we must be careful about is to make the second pit twice as large as the first one."

There was no arguing with this example of Chelmic wisdom, and the workers returned to their digging.

The Steipler and the *Avreich*

A certain *avreich* went to the Steipler Gaon for guidance in learning. After outlining to him how to structure his time by learning for broad general knowledge as well as setting aside time for in-depth analysis, the Steipler remarked, "You sound like a true *masmid*. However, don't forget to help your wife around the house."

The young man tried to deflect the implied *mussar* with an explanation. "My wife is in complete agreement with me that the main thing is my learning. She does not ask for my help, nor does she want it."

The Steipler responded, "That is her mitzva. Your mitzva is to make sure to help around the house. She is your wife…you didn't buy a slave when you married her!"

Rav Eliezer Shach on *Seichel*

A certain young couple was accustomed to going to their parents' home for Shab-bas, alternating between his and her parents every other week. One week the husband was not feeling well, so they decided to stay home and make their own Shabbas. The next week, when the husband was feeling better, he said to his wife, "Last week we did not go to my parents' house, so let's go this week."

"Nor were we at my parents' last week; this week is my parents' turn!" replied his wife. This discussion went on for some time until they decided they would get a third opinion. Who better to field the question than the husband's spiritual guide, Rav Shach?

Upon hearing his *talmid*'s dilemma, the always practical *gadol hador* said to him, "Why don't you stay home for another week and next week you can return to your regular routine…"

Tip 1:
Comedy

Tip 2:
Communication, Conversation

Tip 3:
Common Sense

Tip 4:
Compromise,
Causation

Tip 5:
Caring, Compassion, Courtesy

Tip 6:
Commonality, Compatibility,
Commitment

Tip 7:
Camaraderie, Companionship

I married Miss Right.
I just didn't know her first name
was Always!

"I was married three times," the husband told his new drinking partner, "and all my wives passed away."

"Wow, that's terrible. How did your first wife die?"

"She died from mushroom poisoning."

"Oy! That's a terrible way to die. What happened to your second wife?"

"She also died from mushroom poisoning."

"Oy vey! What a coincidence! Did your third wife also die of mushroom poisoning?"

"No, she died from a broken skull."

"A broken skull? How did that happen?"

"She wouldn't eat her mushrooms!"

My Way or the Highway

An old Jewish couple were having an argument.

Sadie said, "It's Ha-WA-i!"

Morris countered, "No, it's Ha-VA-i!"

Both being extremely stubborn and too proud to look it up, they continued on like this on their way to the grocer's.

On their way they bumped into a stranger and decided to finish it once and for all. Morris addressed him, "Hello, there. Tell me, please. Is it Ha-WA-i or Ha-VA-i?"

The stranger replied, without hesitation, "Ha-VA-i."

Morris smiled triumphantly and said to Sadie, "See, Sadie? Never doubt me." Then he thanked the stranger effusively.

The stranger politely replied, "You're velcome."

You can't drive forward if you're still looking in the rear-view mirror.

The moment a couple stands under the *chuppa* they each take on a new identity, a new destiny, oneness becomes "twoness."

Every *kesuba*, written in Aramaic, leaves a blank for the date to be filled in. And it must be written in Hebrew. That gives you a chance to write the Hebrew word *chodesh* (month), which is similar to *chadash*, the word for "change."

This is a reminder that each partner is beginning *briya chadasha*, life afresh.

Commenting on an unusual Midrash[1] that calls the stage of youth before marriage akin to a "horse," Rav Yechezkel Levenstein, *mashgiach* of Ponovezh Yeshiva in B'nei Brak, explains this odd saying: a youth only sees what he wants, like the proverbial "horse with blinders."

The Midrash is urging those entering marriage to grow past the "horse stage," the infantile self-serving "blinders" of only seeing themselves – and what they want to see.

In one of Charles Schulz's classic *Peanuts* comic strips, Charlie Brown kicks a football, saying, "My grampa and gramma have been married for fifty years..."

---

1. *Koheles Rabba.*

To which his playmate says, "They're lucky, aren't they?" and Charlie replies, "Grampa says it ain't luck…it's skill!"

In the new roles of someone's husband or wife, each spouse faces a daunting array of challenges. To overcome them successfully you need not just will – but, as Charlie puts it, skill!

> The not-too-bright Becky walks into a haberdashery store on Fifth Avenue and says to the salesgirl, "I'd like a pink curtain for my computer screen, please."
>
> "But, madam," the confused salesgirl replies, "computers don't have curtains."
>
> "Well, maybe most don't," Becky says, "but mine's got Windows!"

Skill requires perfecting the nuances of compromise, a word derived from the Latin *compromissum,* a promise to make mutual concessions for conciliation and peace.

There are two halachic terms: *vitur,* which means "concession, giving in," and *peshara,* "compromise." The former describes a situation where a loss is imposed on someone because of the special circumstances, or through generosity or indifference.

The latter, in contrast, comes about by way of shared initiative, a direct agreement between two cooperating parties seeking *shalom.*[2]

Without compromise, the time bomb is ticking. *Shalom bayis* will have a short expiration date on it. Your ideal marriage will become an ordeal marriage. Peace in the home without compromise is an impossible dream, a fantasy, nothing more than wishful thinking.

Here's marital advice from a US president, Lyndon B. Johnson: "I have learned that only two things are necessary to keep one's wife happy. First, let her think she's having her own way. And second, let her have it!"

> An ad was placed in the classifieds section of a newspaper: FOR SALE BY OWNER – Complete set of *Encyclopedia Britannica,* forty-five volumes. Excellent condition. One thousand dollars or best offer. No longer needed. Got married last weekend. Wife knows everything.

---

2.   *Bava Kamma* 9a; *Bava Basra* 15b; *Megilla* 28a; *Sanhedrin* 32b.

Commenting on the major cause of unhappy marriages, Rabbi Yissocher Frand, prolific author and speaker from Ner Israel Rabbinical College, writes, "People are not compromising enough. They are not willing to give in enough."

Rav Frand then quotes Rav Moshe Chafetz, eighteenth-century rabbi and author (*Melechet Machshevet*), that oftentimes "the man is too interested in the *ish* [himself] part of the marriage and not enough in the *isha* [wife] part of the marriage."

Compromise is a skilled art, a *midda* worth perfecting; mastering it fuels successful relationships. And remember: you cannot change another person, you can only change yourself – and, only "according to the effort is the reward"![3]

So keep a watch out for the enemies of compromise: domination, family power games, stubborness. As the Yiddishists say: Mountains do not meet, only people do!

> My wife and I have a perfectly compatible marriage. I don't
> try to run her life – and I don't try to run mine!

A stubborn spouse is a contradiction of Torah terms. Stubborn equals intolerable; unbudging is unbearable.

Remember: the home that acts as an exemplary role model of *shalom bayis* becomes a tangible springboard for peace in all of Israel. So take the initiative, be proactive, and more demanding of yourself, not of your spouse.

There's no need to always be right and rigid; try to be flexible and supple instead of insisting and unrelenting. The best weapon of *shalom bayis*? Large doses of spontaneous adapatability!

If you don't have the DNA to compromise, if you can't "surrender" to *seichel*, logic, maturity, the first victim is *shalom bayis*; it completely disintegrates in the face of spousal inflexibility.

---

3. *Pirkei Avos* 5:22; Saadia HaGaon, *Emunos V'deios* 933:2. After the Flood, the first time the dove returned it came back empty-handed in its search for dry land. The Torah says that the bird returned "to the ark," and not "into the ark." The commentators explain that the dove, afraid because it had failed in its mission, would not be allowed back into the ark. Noah thus took the dove and brought the bird back into the ark, a recognition of the effort, and not its actual realization. The general consensus in the Talmud is this: if you go to the effort but are prevented by unforeseen circumstances from completing a mitzva, you still get the credit for the mitzva.

In fact, the fastest route to living "happily never after" is the self-destructive ultimatum, the I'm-not-budging philosophy of individualism that tolls the death bell for compatibility.

Or as the pop folk singers croon, "I'm 'a do things my way/It's my way/My way, or the highway!"

You cannot control a relationship with this harsh attitude any more than a barometer can control the weather.

Compare this to the compassionate and protective Arba Turim code of Jewish law, which requires a husband to give his wife *ahava, kavod, rachamim* and *shmira* (love, honor, mercy, guarding).

Or compare it to the Rambam, who calmly codifies the steps necessary to lead couples to a "beautiful and praiseworthy" relationship: Husbands must speak gently to their wives, buy them gifts "within their means," make them feel happy and comfortable, never show depression, etc. A wife must be modest, never pain her husband, stay attractive, etc.[4]

In other words: You want *shalom bayis*? Work at it!

> One day, Betty goes to her dentist and asks him how much it will cost to extract a wisdom tooth.
>
> "A hundred dollars," the dentist replies.
>
> "Wow, that's a lot. Isn't there a cheaper way?"
>
> "Well, if I don't use an anaesthetic, I can knock it down to eighty dollars."
>
> "No, no! That's still way too expensive."
>
> "OK. Well, if I save on anaesthesia and simply rip the teeth out with a pair of plain pliers, I could get away with charging only forty dollars."
>
> "Hmmm. That's a bit better, but still too much."
>
> "OK. Well, if I let one of my inexperienced first-year intern students with shaky hands do it without anaesthetic and use the old rusty pliers, I could do it for you for fifteen dollars."
>
> "Great! Book my husband Moishie in for next Tuesday morning!"

4.   Rambam, *Hilchos Ishus* 15:17–20.

The Rambam, master of *seichel* and rationality, also throws in an indispensable word of common sense: "Do things in moderation, never in the extreme…until they become a fixed habit!"[5]

Adds Yehuda ben Ilai: "The way of life is like a path between two forbidden roads, one of fire and one of ice. The slightest bend in either direction is fatal. What should one do? Let him walk in the middle of the road!"[6]

Remember: the letters of the Torah are divided into three sizes: large, medium, and small.[7] The Torah itself was written with medium letters, to indicate that a Jew, in his attitudes, should follow the medium path.[8]

There are no quick-fix, short-cut, extreme solutions. You can't "microwave" the building blocks of a relationship (as they say: you only get one chance at a second chance!). Taking your time is the fastest way to a healthy marriage. Moderation and patience are the *shalom bayis* forces of nature that control the harvest.

One day, a procession of three horse-drawn wagons of hay trotted past Rav Yosef Dov Soloveitchik, the brilliant great-grandson of Rabbi Chaim Volozhiner and author of *Beis Halevi*, as he was walking with his students, prompting him to note that "the horse pulling the third wagon is eating hay from the wagon in front of him. The lead horse has nothing to eat from, but benefits from the fact that the second horse eats from his wagon, thereby lightening his load. The middle horse benefits the most, since his load is being diminished by the third horse, and he gets to eat from the wagon of the first horse. This scene supports the idea that either extreme of anything is rarely beneficial."

Moderation ensures normality, normality ensures calm and consistency, which, in turn, gives *shalom bayis* a chance to grow.

Just because you can doesn't mean you should! The ancient Greeks called it *meden agan* (nothing in excess)! Knowing where the boundaries are is called… *seichel*!

---

5.   Rambam, *Hilchos Deios*, 1:4, 7.

6.   Tosafos, *Chagiga* 2:6.

7.   Jewish education begins with a child at age five learning *Vayikra*, "And God called," whose first letter (*aleph*) is smaller than the other letters to stress the humility of Moshe (Shach, *Yoreh Deah* 245:8; *Sefer Chassidim* 740).

8.   Rambam, *Hilchos Deios* 1:4.

> After getting engaged, Esther goes to her *rebbetzin*, who tells her, "Just remember, the first ten years are the hardest."
>> "How long have you been married?"
>> "Ten years!"

If you go into a marriage unable to compromise you are already carrying excess baggage. Your path will be *krum* (crooked); *shalom bayis* will not even be a blip on your marital radar. Moderate and patient couples are usually less intense, less violent, less rash.

Compromise is that little hole at the top of your pressure cooker. Block it and your marriage will implode. Use it often and your *shalom bayis* will be satisfyingly obvious.

The Ponovezher Rav went out of his way to avoid arguments. He explained why:

> Years ago the *Chofetz Chaim* told me that I would be successful in virtually all of my endeavors except in disputes that might arise. He assured me that, however hard I tried, I would never win an argument. Therefore, it is my practice never to allow myself to even get involved in one!

The entire Torah is an effort to foster a religious culture of humility, self-restraint and moderation, one that allows each Jew to *intuitively* respect the integrity of others, especially a spouse.

> A little girl asks her mother, "How did the human race appear?"
>
> "Well," the mother replies, "God made Adam and Chava and they had children and so was all mankind made."
>
> Later, the girl asks her more free-thinking father the same question.
>
> "Well," the father answers, "Many years ago there were monkeys from which the human race evolved."
>
> The girl is now confused so she asks her mother, "How come you told me the human race was created by God, and Daddy said they developed from monkeys?"
>
> "Well," the mother replied, "it's very simple. I told you about my side of the family – and your father told you about his!"

It's simple: *shalom bayis* is contingent upon the total absence of egocentricity.

Let's try *gematria*: the value of the Hebrew word for "found" (*matza*) is the same as the word for "humility" (*anava),* implying that humility is a prerequisite to finding, *and keeping,* one's spouse.

And if you haven't found your spouse yet, if you've gone out with a hundred different people "and still aren't married," suggests Dr. Aaron Mandel, "you must consider the possibility that what you need is not to meet more people, but to become a new person!"[9]

The Midrash Rabba quotes Yehuda Hanasi (*Rebbi*), a key Torah leader in Judea toward the end of the second century and editor of the Mishna, as saying that peace is so great that it can spare the lives of even the worst transgressors ("If there is peace among them," God admits, "I cannot harm them"). And so the generation of Babel, greater sinners than the generation of the Flood, were spared. Why? Because they were at least unified.

Whenever Rav Yehuda's wife would lose her temper, her husband replied in a kind, courteous and polite manner.[10]

Rav Yaakov Kamanetsky always advised restraint in life, and taught that self-control required finding the middle ground where both sides can meet in peace. The Baal Shem Tov sought a state of *zerizus metinus*, "agility with moderation," which is knowledge "with modesty."

"People talk about the middle of the road as though it were unacceptable," observed Dwight D. Eisenhower. But "things are not all black and white…. The middle of the road is all of the usable surface. The extremes, right and left, are in the gutters."

Or, as the Yiddishists of Eastern Europe put it: You can't control the wind, but you can adjust your sails!

> Isaac is sitting quietly reading a document for a long time which piques his wife's interest.
> "*Nu*, Isaac, what are you reading?" she asks.
> "Our *kesuba*."
> "Our *kesuba*? Why are you staring at our *kesuba* for nearly an hour?"
> "I'm looking for something."
> "What?"
> "A loophole!"

9. The *Jewish Observer*, April 1996.
10. *Yevamos* 63b.

Aaron Hacohen is known as the ultimate marriage counselor par excellence. Why? The *Chasam Sofer* explains that Aaron's love of peace motivated him to calmly solve marital problems by finding common ground between the parties.

Aaron's obsession with peace motivated him to walk through the entire camp of Israel every day seeking to promote harmony between husbands and wives, neighbors, adversaries.

This exceptional concern for *shalom* is why the entire people of Israel mourned him for thirty days instead of just the traditional seven, and why Hillel advised Jews to "be a disciple of Aaron,"[11] the courageous peacemaker.[12]

When the Torah states that the *entire* House of Israel – men and women alike – mourned the passing of Aaron, it is contrasting this outpouring to that for Moshe, whose passing was mourned only by the men. Rashi explains that both men and women appreciated Aaron's peacekeeping efforts equally.[13]

A master of interpersonal relations, Aaron would go to one of the parties arguing and say, "Your friend feels bad that the two of you are fighting. He is ashamed for wronging you. He told me he loves you but doesn't know what to say to apologize."

Aaron would then go to the other side and say the same.

Eventually, all their enmity disappeared. Each would respond, "How can I remain in a fight with one so beloved to me?" – and rush and embrace the other with no words being spoken.[14]

Aaron knew that in the absence of harmony, material blessings were meaningless, and that one blessing of peace equaled all other blessings combined.[15]

"Whoever makes peace in his home," writes the Midrash, "is as one who made peace between each Jew and every other Jew."[16]

Aaron understood the disastrous chronology of events: no peace, no blessings, no Torah. So did Rabbeinu Yona.

The Sage thought it a good idea for a *kehilla* to hire loving, caring, cheerful,

---

11.   *Bamidbar* 20:28-29; *Pirkei d'Rabbi Eliezer* 17; *Pirkei Avos* 1:12.
12.   Ironically, because the three-week period of mourning for the destruction of the Temples is a time of national introspection, the anniversary of Aaron's death seems to slip by unnoticed.
13.   Rashi, *Devarim* 34:8.
14.   *Avos d'Rabbi Nosson* 12.
15.   Rashi, *Vayikra* 26:6.
16.   *Avos d'Rabbi Nosson* 28.

kindhearted people with the talent to appease others and send them out to promote peace among Jews. Their payment would not just be monetary. The Talmud defines the reward: a guaranteed spot in *Olam Haba!*[17]

Adds the *Tiferes Yisroel*: it's one's duty to try to bring peace between two people – *even* if they're *not* interested![18]

> The visiting *rav* is giving his Shabbas *drasha* on *middos* and ends with a rhetorical question to his audience: "Is there anybody here who thinks he is perfect?"
>
> The congregants are in deep thought, when, slowly, Moishie in the back stands up.
>
> The *rav*, surprised, asks, "*Nu*, and why do you stand? Do you think you are perfect?"
>
> "Oh, no," he replies, "I'm not perfect at all. I'm just standing in memory of my wife's first husband who was."

For the sake of *shalom bayis*, can one compromise on Torah issues?[19] (This is a complicated issue and you must see a *rav*. No two cases are alike. I know a couple who divorced over religious differences. He thought he was God –and she didn't!) In general, you should not, but before you get overly dogmatic on micro issues of Torah, remember the Ramban's *vort*: better to act in the spirit rather than the letter of the law!

In a famous decision, the thirteenth-century Spanish sage explains how it's possible in everyday life to keep every mitzva in the Torah and still miss the point of "holiness." So what to do? In relations between man and woman, the Ramban relied on the Torah's admonition that "Thou shalt do that which is upright and good."

---

17. *Taanis* 24a.
18. *Pe'ah* 1:1.
19. Rabbi Moshe Isserles reminds us that, under certain conditions, such as maintaining *shalom* and human dignity, one can even get married on Shabbas: "It is best to not perform the wedding on the Sabbath, but when there is ground for concern that if the wedding is not performed the match will be jeopardized or the bride will be shamed – under such circumstances, he who is lenient has done no harm. The good deed that he has done will outweigh for him any wrongness if his intention was for the sake of peace" (*She'eilos U'teshuvos HaRama*, Number 125).

Torah linguists take the word *ma'agal* from Shlomo Hamelech's "In the way of wisdom I instructed you, I directed you on the straight paths (*ma'aglei yashar*),"[20] and point out that it can either mean a "path" or a "circle." This "straight circle" is obviously an inherent contradiction: a line is straight, a circle is round!

What Shlomo Hamelech means to say is that the direction of a Torah way of life needs to be balanced, so that you "close the circle" on life.

Here's an example: Rav Yosef Shlomo Kahanamen, the Ponovezher Rav, was puzzled by a statement by the Rosh, "One should not speak between washing his hands for bread and the blessing over bread, and one should greet everyone with a warm *shalom*."[21]

Why express two separate *halachos* in the same sentence?

Although it's best to remain silent between washing hands and eating, what happens if a guest walks in and extends his hand in greeting?

By juxtaposing these two circumstances, we can read the Rosh's verse to mean, "One should not speak between washing his hands for bread and the blessing over bread *unless* he must greet another person with a warm *shalom*."

In other words, the risk of insulting another, of not promoting peace among Jews, in conformity with the mitzva of *bein adam l'chaveiro*, supercedes the required halachic silence between washing and eating.[22]

This is a healthy attitude, explains Rashi, not standing upon "rights" but compromising "beyond the letter of the law" in the interests of a higher Torah morality.

> A little old Jewish lady gets onto a crowded bus and stands in front of a seated young girl. Holding her hand to her chest, she says to the girl, "If you knew what I have, you would give me your seat." The girl gets up and gives her seat to the old lady.
>
> It's a hot day. The girl takes out a fan and starts fanning herself.
>
> The woman looks up and says, "If you knew what I have, you would give me that fan." The girl gives her the fan, too.
>
> Fifteen minutes later the woman gets up and says to the

20.   *Mishlei* 4:11.
21.   *Orchos Chaim l'Rosh* 21.
22.   Tur, *Orach Chaim* 166.

bus driver, "Stop, I want to get off here." The bus driver tells her he has to drop her at the next corner, not in the middle of the block. With her hand across her chest, she tells the driver, "If you knew what I have, you would let me off the bus right here."

The bus driver pulls over and opens the door to let her out. As she's walking out of the bus, he asks, "Madam, what is it you have?"

She looks back and says, nonchalantly, "Chutzpa!"

The Ponovezher Rav's application of the Rosh's insight equally applies to marriage: no relationship can be declared sanctified (*kiddushin*, the marriage ceremony, derives from the same root as *kodesh*, "holy") and sustain itself absent the spirit of, for example, mutual honor and respect.

Something can be technically permissible when viewed alone, explained Rav Shimon Schwab, a major follower of Rav Shimshon Raphael Hirsch's philosophy of *Torah im Derech Eretz*, but can be, in the final analysis, a Torah prohibition because of the mitzva of *kedoshim tihiyu*, the commandment "to be holy."[23]

Remember: you were married *k'das Moshe v'Yisroel*, "according to the laws of Moshe and Israel," which includes such non-explicit Torah requirements as authenticity, dignity, appreciation and self-worth.[24]

The Talmud uses a verse in Tehillim[25] ("It is time to work for the Lord; they have made void your Torah") as scriptural license to legislate against overt Torah laws – in order to *uphold* the Torah.

In the days of the Torah, there was a system of checks and balances that applied between the Jewish courts and the king of Israel. The rabbis on the courts

---

23.   Tosafos explain that certain people learn Torah for such selfish motives as arrogance (for example, trying to beat others in debates on halacha). The Rambam says that another form of selfishness is learning Torah just to be respected and to be called "Rabbi." Rav Yisroel Salanter makes the stunning accusation that some learn Torah to be better able to steal from others. When discussing the respect one should give to his *rav*, the Rama says this is not absolute. It depends on whether that *rav* taught "practical halacha" – i.e., how to conduct yourself as a *mensch* (*Shulchan Aruch, Yoreh Deah* 242:30).

24.   *Sefer Hachinuch* 13, 341; *Yevamos* 62b, *Sanhedrin* 76b; *Bava Metzia* 59a, Rambam, *Hilchos Ishus* 15:19; *Chullin* 84b; *Hilchos Deios* 5:10.

25.   *Brachos* 63; *Tehillim* 119:126.

upheld the strict letter of the law, while the mandate of the monarch was to uphold the spirit of the law. This dichotomy created a "balanced whole," a climate of compromise.

To prevent the king from abusing this power, he had to carry a *sefer Torah* with him at all times, a constant reminder of what was at stake. When the monarchy was abolished, the courts wore two hats: upholders of *both* the letter and the spirit of the law. This led to the custom that, after finishing a case, the judges would turn to each other and ask, "Was justice served?" and then reexamine their decision to make sure it was rendered in the spirit of the law as well.

In fact, it is not only possible to use the proper tools of Jewish law and arrive at the wrong conclusion, but violating the spirit of Torah is seen as worse than rigid fidelity to the Torah.

Rav Yochanan makes the startling accusation that strict adherence to Jewish law can be destructive: "Jerusalem was destroyed only because they acted in accordance with the letter of the Torah and did not go beyond it!"[26]

> Bernie and Chana decide to discuss their *shalom bayis* problems with their rabbi. Sitting in the rabbi's study, Bernie complains that they are not on the same religious level.
>
> "What do you mean?" the *rav* asks. "I assume you at least keep the Ten Commandments?"
>
> "Oh, yes," Chana replies.
>
> "Well, at least that's good to hear," the rabbi sighs.
>
> "Yes," adds Bernie, "she keeps six of them and I keep the other four."

In a response to a letter from a husband whose wife had become less Orthodox, the seventh Lubavitcher Rebbe urged him not to break the marriage and family over it, and emphasized that maintaining *shalom bayis* has traditionally superseded concerns over an unequal balance of religiosity between husband and wife.

In his sefer *Nesivos Olam*, Rabbi Yehuda Loew of Prague (*Maharal*) asks: "What, in one word, is the essence of the man-woman relationship?" He answers, *emuna*, the art of mutual faith and trust. He is influenced by a Gemora, itself based on a Midrash, which convinces him that *shalom bayis* is achieved when

---

26. *Bava Metzia* 30b.

each side can "faithfully trust" the other party not to descend to lower spiritual levels over the years.[27]

Rav Yisroel Salanter, *mussar* master and expert in human nature, advised his followers never to make another person's spirituality their own religious "cause." He had a famous line: "The other person's spirituality is your materialism – and the other person's materialism is your spirituality!"

In a marriage context, this means when you compromise and let your spouse's needs come first, this fulfills *your* spiritual need, not your spouse's!

Even Avraham, notes the Midrash,[28] urges God to compromise ("Thou must forgo a little") in his presentation on absolute justice. And Rav Aharon Kotler, Torah giant from Lakewood, was convinced that selfish people, starting by worrying about themselves, eventually deteriorate to wanting to deprive others of *their* needs.

Selfless and sensitive folks, claims Moshe Chaim Luzzato, the seventeenth-century Italian kabbalist and writer of ethics, "will always try to give others a good feeling."[29]

"Spouses have to be like astronauts," one psychiatrist observed, "always making mid-course corrections." Benjamin Franklin was more blunt: Keep your eyes wide open before marriage, half shut afterwards!

An inability to compromise shows the ugly side of one's character. Conceit and arrogance beget rigidity, obstinacy and intransigence.

If you are perfectionistic, critical and judgmental, beware of the *chuppa*! Why? Because marriage is another word for meeting another halfway. If such terms as "concession" and "middle ground" are not in your vocabulary, then any attempt at achieving *shalom bayis* is a waste of time, an exercise in futility.

Abbaye Keshisha the Elder said, "Discord is like a plank on a bridge; once it is firm, it remains firm." Rashi agrees: "New planks on a bridge are wobbly; with time, the planks settle into place and become firm."

Similarly, frequent discord becomes habitual!

In his book of Hebrew poetry, Shem Tov Falaquera, the thirteenth-century Torah philosopher, gave these words of wisdom: "Always adapt thyself to time and circumstance."

---

27. *Taanis* 8a.
28. *Bereishis Rabba* 39:6.
29. M.C. Luzzato, *Mesilas Yesharim* 19.

The Jewish home is no place for dogmatism, nor one's ego. No one ever "has all the answers."

Patience is the deposit on the policy, and compromise is the premium for marriage insurance, the most potent umbrella to protect against a rocky relationship and a rained-on marriage.

> "*Nu*, what's the problem?" the *rav* asks Sylvia.
> "It's my husband, Hymie. I need a divorce."
> "Why? What happened?"
> "I need a divorce for religious reasons!"
> "Religious reasons?!"
> "Yes. I worship money – and Hymie has none!"

Remember: the *mezuza* is placed on an angle[30] as a compromise solution between those who argued it should be vertical (Rashi) and others who said it should be horizontal (Tosefos).

Since it's the first thing you see when you enter your home, it's a constant reminder: a happy home requires you to bend and compromise.

Marriage means sharing; sharing means joint decisions. Joint decisions leave no room for conceit, smugness or self-importance. If *shalom bayis* needed a motto it would be, "If it's important to you, it's important to me, because you are important to me!"

As they say, if you pull a rope too taut it is likely to break. And just watch the weathervane. If it insists on staying still, it will be smashed by the first storm. Only its ability to turn with the wind keeps it alive and well.

Or as the Yiddishists would say: Not only is half a loaf better than no bread, it's oftentimes better than a whole loaf!

"Pride goes before destruction!" warns Ben Sira, and, as the Talmud reminds us, "It is meritorious to compromise."[31]

Those who insist on having their way are usually consistent. They can't differentiate between important issues and the insignificant, petty and trivial.

They are oblivious to that wise Yiddish proverb: Far better to bend a little than to break it all! This expression is adopted from a Midrash: "He who attempts to resist the wave is swept away, but he who bends before it abides!" – to which

---

30. Shulchan Aruch, *Yoreh Deah* 289:6.
31. Yehoshua ben Korcha, Tosefta: *Sanhedrin* 1:3.

the Talmud adds: "A man afflicted with haughtiness will be disturbed by the slightest breeze!"[32]

Scratch the surface in any home that lacks *shalom bayis* and chances are you will find at least one stubborn spouse. Insisting on being the boss is the surest recipe for marital disaster.

Never forget: compromise is not a sign of weakness, nor is give-and-take an admission of defeat. Compromise is a virtue. Concession shows wisdom, maturity and self-confidence.

And more important: willingness to compromise is a sign to your spouse that you are also sensitive to his or her opinion.

> The newlywed couple are watching a popular magic show and are amazed at a trick the magician has just done. The excited husband stands up and yells out, "Hey! How'd ya do that?"
>
> "I can't tell you," the magician shouts back into the audience. "It's a secret. If I tell ya, I'd have to kill ya!"
>
> The husband sits down, thinks for a few moments, then stands back up and shouts, "OK! Let's compromise! Just tell my wife!"

---

32.   *Vayikra Rabba* 44:15; *Sota* 5a.

The Vizhnitz Rebbe, *Shalom Bayis* and Jewelry

The *Damesek Eliezer* of Vizhnitz, Rabbi Eliezer Hager, was once walking through the streets of Tel Aviv accompanied by a chassid by the name of Reb Dov Waltzer. As the two passed a jewelry store, the Rebbe suddenly stopped short and motioned to Reb Dov to do the same.

To Reb Dov's great surprise, Rav Eliezer entered the jewelry store. He asked to see a selection of a certain type of jewelry. The owners were very courteous, showing him various samples of expensive jewelry. Rav Eliezer spent a few minutes examining the choices and inquiring about the price of each one. Finally, he chose one piece of jewelry and paid for it.

Reb Dov was astounded. Since when did the Rebbe go shopping for jewelry? And why had he chosen this particular store? He wanted to ask the Rebbe but he held back, lest the question sound disrespectful.

The Rebbe must have sensed his chassid's puzzlement, because he turned to his companion and said, "You must surely be wondering why I entered the store and purchased a piece of jewelry."

Reb Dov looked at the Rebbe expectantly. Yes, that was exactly what he was wondering!

"As we passed the jewelry shop," the Rebbe explained, "I heard loud voices raised in anger. I understood that the married owners were having a serious argument. You know how it is when two people are in the heat of anger – they say things they later regret. I wanted to interrupt the argument before it escalated into a full-blown fight and give the couple a chance to calm down. My tactic worked. As soon as I entered the store, the shouting stopped as the husband and wife hurried to serve me. Since it is forbidden to inquire about something one has no intention of purchasing [that would constitute the prohibition of *onaa*], I purchased the piece of jewelry."

Rav Avrohom Pam on Compromise

Adam Harishon is described as an ingrate by Chazal for blaming his wife for having fed him the forbidden fruit ("The woman that You gave me – she offered me the fruit...," as if the fault lies with the "*Shadchan*"). He had forgotten how he had searched among all the creatures of the world for a mate, to no avail, and he had forgotten how, when God put him to sleep and created Chava and brought her to him, his joy knew no bounds, and he exclaimed ecstatically, "This time, a bone from my bones, flesh from my flesh – this shall be called 'woman'!"

The joy was forgotten in the rush of incrimination. So, too, in many a marriage, when minor differences arise, one partner tends to magnify the problem and fault the spouse for the problem.

In a moment of anger, he can deeply hurt the very person to whom he owes so much, overlooking all of the joy and happiness his spouse has brought him over the years. This is the ultimate in ingratitude.

– Rav Avrohom Pam, *zt"l, rosh yeshiva* Mesivta Torah Vodaas

The Peacekeepers

It is a mitzva to appoint peacekeepers in a community who will help maintain peace between spouses or any other community members. They should be pleasant, caring people who understand the human psyche and can help those involved in a dispute reach a peaceful solution. Ideally, they should also be tough enough to force uncooperative people to cooperate.

As the Gemora asserts in *Maseches Taanis*, anyone who can instill or restore peace between people in a loving, cheerful manner is guaranteed a place in *Olam Haba*.

– Rabbeinu Yona, *Igeres Hateshuva*

A *Yerushalmi* Compromises for *Shalom Bayis*

An esteemed *Yerushalmi* who was close to the Brisker Rav baked matzos with him and guarded them carefully. But when his wife was cleaning the house for Pesach she took the matzos down from a closet and her young son opened the box and began handling the matza. The wife's heart sank. Who knew whether the child's hands were clean or not? Afraid to tell her husband, she decided to ask her brother-in-law to get other matzos from another *chabura* and put them in the box (after cleaning it).

On *erev* Pesach her husband immediately realized that his matzos had been swapped with others but to avoid tension he pretended not to have noticed.

His wife felt pangs of conscience and on Seder night she told him what had happened.

"I noticed," he replied, "but I thought it would be better to be *machmir* concerning anger and *shalom bayis* rather than be *machmir* about matzos!"

Rabbi Eliezer Papo on *Shalom Bayis*

If peace between man and his friend is so important, how much more so is this true between man and his wife. It is not enough that we, ourselves, be cordial and amiable – we must strive to help others be the same way. If one hears about an argument between two people or between a couple, he should do whatever he can to help them solve their problems and bring about peace between them, since this is a great source of pleasure for his Creator.

– Rabbi Eliezer Papo

The Blessing of Peace

The tractates of *Brachos, Nazir, Yevamos* and *Krisos*, as well as the Shabbas night and day prayer services, end with the following narrative.

> Rabbi Elazar said in the name of Rabbi Chanina: Sages multiply peace in the world, as it says, "And all of your sons (*banayich*) are disciples of God and the peace of your sons (*banayich*) will be abundant."[33]
>
> Do not read "*banayich* (your sons)," but rather "*bonayich* (your builders)."
>
> "Those who sincerely love Your Torah have abundant peace and they do not stumble in sin. Let there be peace in your walls and tranquility in your palaces. For the sake of my brothers and friends I will wish you peace. God will bless His people with peace."[34]

---

33. *Yeshayahu* 54:13.
34. *Tehillim* 119:165, 122:7–9, 29:11.

You Have Nothing!

The Gerer Rebbe was prepared to do just about anything for the sake of peace. When it came to ensuring peace, no amount of effort and no price was considered excessive. Time and again he would forgo his own honor both privately and publicly in order to increase the level of harmony among people.

On one occasion the Rebbe said to one of his brothers-in-law, "I was put into this world in order to encourage peace." As well, in a letter to a rabbi in the United States whose community was involved in an intense conflict, he wrote, "If you don't have peace, you have nothing."

The Rebbe maintained that one should yield to others for the sake of peace. He often encouraged his followers to make far-reaching concessions to others even if they considered these concessions unreasonable. "Nothing is unreasonable when done in order to maintain peace. *Chazal* have taught, 'Great is peace, despised is conflict.'"

God and Peace

Shalom bayis is one of the main spiritual tasks the Torah sets for us in life (*ikar habirurim shelo*). When the opposite (i.e., divorce) occurs, "the Altar in the Holy Temple sheds tears." In other words, *machlokes* in a family is not just a private affair, but has a significant impact at the cosmic level where prayers are heard for the peace of *the entire Jewish people.*

The procedure prescribed for testing an alleged *sota* (a woman suspected of adultery) was to write a series of curses that included the name of God and to subsequently erase the words in water. If, after drinking the water, the woman remained unharmed, then she would reunite with her husband. Our Sages point out that God allowed His name to be erased in order to bring a husband and wife back together, thus illustrating the great importance of *shalom bayis*, harmony in the home.[35]

The Maharal suggests that God permits His name to be erased for the sake of bringing about peace between husband and wife because God's Shechina rests upon a peaceful marriage. It is therefore worthwhile to erase the written form of God's Name since, by reconciling the couple, we are, in effect, enabling God's presence to rest between them. Harmony among Jews is so important that the mitzva "to bring about peace between man and his fellow" is one of the few mitzvos for which a person is rewarded in this world while his principal reward awaits him in the World to Come.[36]

---

35. *Bamidbar Rabba* 5:23.
36. *Pe'ah* 1:1.

Reb Rafael of Barshad Works Toward Peace

Reb Rafael of Barshad made great efforts to make peace between quarreling parties – husbands and wives, business partners, friends who had a falling-out. On Tisha b'Av, he came to the home of a man who had been involved in a quarrel with another man to try to patch things up.

"Rebbe," said the man, "must this be done today? Can't it wait for tomorrow?"

"On the contrary," said Reb Rafael, "the *Beis Hamikdash* was destroyed on this very day because of *sinas chinam* (baseless hatred). It is therefore particularly important to work toward bringing peace between Jews today!"

Rav Shlomo Zalman Auerbach on the Household's *Shechina*

One day a friend was accompanying Rav Shlomo Zalman Auerbach. As they approached his home, Rav Shlomo Zalman suddenly began busying himself with his appearance, straightening his coat, doing up his buttons, and making sure he looked neat.

His friend, confused, asked, "What was that all about?"

Rav Shlomo Zalman replied, "According to the Gemora, when a husband and wife live together in peace, the *Shechina* dwells with them. Since I am about to come home, I am making myself presentable for the *Shechina*."

Tip 1:
Comedy

Tip 2:
Communication, Conversation

Tip 3:
Common Sense

Tip 4:
Compromise, Causation

Tip 5:
Caring, Compassion, Courtesy

Tip 6:
Commonality, Compatibility, Commitment

Tip 7:
Camaraderie, Companionship

Choose your love,
then love your choice!

One afternoon Max comes home from work to find total mayhem. His two young children are in the front garden, half-naked, soaking wet and playing with the garden hose. There is food all over the lawn, rubbish spilled everywhere and some of the plants have been pulled up and are lying on the path. The front door to his house is wide open.

As Max goes inside, he finds an even bigger mess. The nest of tables are lying on their sides, all the vases have been knocked over and wet flowers are on the floor, the armchair cushions are lying where they were thrown and one of the children has been sick over the carpet. The children's room is strewn inches deep with toys and various items of clothing.

Max goes into the kitchen and finds the sink full of unwashed dishes from the morning's breakfast. None of the food has been cleared up and the fridge door is wide open. He's quite worried by now and heads up the stairs to look for his wife Fay. He has to step over yet more toys and piles of clothes as water trickles under the bathroom door and into the hall. He peers inside and sees wet towels, spilled bath oils, his shaver lying on the floor and toothpaste smeared everywhere. He turns off the bath tap and rushes to his bedroom. There he finds Fay, curled up in bed, still in her pajamas and reading a book. She smiles at him and says, "How did your day go, dear?"

"My day?" Max says, bewildered. "What happened here today?!"

"Well," she smiles, "you know every day when you come home from work and you ask me what in the world did I do today?"

"Yes."

"Well, today I didn't do it!"

Middos 'n Manners

An efficiency expert is giving a class and says, "You know, at home, for the first five years of my marriage I watched my wife spend ten minutes each night *schlepping* out the garbage. Then one night I told her, 'You know, honey, it would be much quicker if you used bigger trash bags and then you wouldn't have to make so many trips.'"

A student asks, "Did it work? Did it save time?"

"Oh, sure," he replies. "Instead of ten minutes, I now do it in five!"

So, who's in charge of *shalom bayis*?

Pirkei d'Rabbi Eliezer tells us the woman sets the standards in the home.

To prove the wife's influence, the Midrash describes a couple who divorced and went their separate ways. Both of them remarried. One married a wicked man (*rasha*) and turned her husband into a *tzadik*; the other man's new wife was herself evil (*merushaas*), and turned her good husband into a *rasha*.

"If he is worthy, she is a helpmate; if he is unworthy, she is not," observed Talmudic Sage Eleazar ben Pedat.[1]

Rav Yisroel Salanter, explaining the inherent contradiction in the term *ezer kenegdo*, "a helpmate, opposite," says that sometimes a wife's help (*ezer*) can lead to her husband's downfall (*kenegdo*), and sometimes her opposition (*kenegdo*) can end up being a big help (*ezer*).

It is the wife, notes ben Sira, that prevents man from turning into a "vagabond" ("Without a hedge the vineyard is laid waste; and without a wife, a man is a homeless wanderer!").

Another Midrash looks at the wives of Korach and Onn ben Peles.

The former was a prime supporter-instigator of her husband's rebellion against Moshe and Aaron; the latter's wife convinced her husband not to follow Korach's insurrection. Both husbands listened to their wives. Korach died; Onn was spared.

---

1.   *Yevamos* 63a.

> The Jewish boy from Brooklyn wants to become an actor so he flies out to Hollywood and starts auditioning. After six months he calls home excitedly and tells his mom, "Mom, wish me mazel tov! I got accepted! I got a role in a movie!"
>
> "What part are you playing?"
>
> "I'm playing the part of a Jewish husband!"
>
> "Oh," she replies. "Next time, try to get a speaking role!"

Traditionally, the Jewish woman is the "foundation" of the home, the *akeres habayis*, the crucial component to stability, continuity, strength and wisdom.

She remains the emotional and spiritual thermostat ("*tzofia halichos beisa*"), determines the household *ruach* (character and atmosphere), sets the *derech* (direction and tone) of the *chinuch* (education) of the children, holds the keys to family unity, and plays a decisive role in interfamily relationships between parents and children, children and children, and the two parents.

The husband and children find not just comfort and warmth at home after the pressures of a hard day, whether at school or at business, but inspiration and strength to continue on to the next day.

Women are thus known as *Beis Yaakov*, wherein the word *beis*, meaning "house," alludes also to *bas*, "daughter." It is the woman who fortifies the home with spirituality; "*Chochmas nashim bansa baisa* (The wisdom of women built their houses)."

> Mimi and Zissy, both young girls in the dating period, were complaining to each other as to the quality of the boys they meet. "Why," says Mimi, "just the other day I met a guy and from the very first minute, he was screaming and cursing at me!"
>
> "Wow! That's awful. How did you meet him?"
>
> "I accidentally ran over him with my car."

The term the Torah uses when Eve is created from the body of Adam is *vayiven*, from the verb *bana*, "and He built."

From the fact that *vayiven* comes from the root *bina* (wisdom), our Sages deduced that women were given more wisdom (*bina yeseira*) than men. Therefore, since girls grow up faster than boys, their maturity date (bas mitzva) comes a year earlier, at twelve, than boys, whose bar mitzva is at thirteen.[2]

Rabbi Yose, whom Rashi describes as a plain-speaking sage, never called his wife his "wife" but his "home,"[3] because she was the central *ikkar* ("essence") of his life.[4]

A cab driver once asked Rav Aryeh Levin, the *tzadik* of Jerusalem, "Where's your house?" He got no reply. So the driver asked him where his street was, to which Rav Aryeh replied, "From the day my wife died, I no longer have a house. I only have a street."

Remember: Elisha had the attribute of prophecy and yet he still followed the advice of his wife![5]

And before Rabbi Elazar ben Azaria,[6] contemporary of Rabbi Akiva, accepted the extraordinarily important position of *nasi* ("religious president"), he first went home to get his wife's opinion.[7]

Avraham might have achieved a high level of prophecy but even so God advised him to listen to Sarah for her understanding (his wife's prophecy was on a higher level than his).

A "house" is a perfect analogy for marriage: if the foundation is strong (*values*), and its cornerstone is peace and harmony (*shalom bayis*), it can remain

---

2.   *Bereishis* 2:22; *Nidda* 45b.

3.   *Shabbas* 118b.

4.   The homely term "hospitality" comes from the Latin word of feminine tense, *hospes*, meaning either "host" or "guest" (and leading to "hospice," "hostel," "hotel," and "hospital," a word which originally referred to an inn, and then to a refuge for the homeless and sick, all connoting the warm welcome that women give to the "stranger"). The word *ushpizin*, which means "guest" in medieval Aramaic, a reference to the *Zohar* tradition that seven Biblical patriarchs (Avraham, Yitzchak, Yaakov, Yosef, Moshe, Aaron, David) visit Jews (invisibly) over Succos, also comes from the same Latin word for "hospitality."

5.   *Brachos* 61a.

6.   "One who talks the talk without walking the walk," to paraphrase Rabbi Elazar, "is like a big tree with lots of leaves but no roots. The first strong wind to blow will uproot it and throw it on its face. He who walks the walk more than he talks the talk is like a tree with few leaves but lots of roots. All the ill winds in the universe won't move it from its place, but it doesn't provide much shade."

7.   *Brachos* 27b.

standing for decades; and if time and energy (*respect, kavod, modesty, friendship, caring*, etc.) are invested in its maintenance, it is secure for life.

> Benjamin is having breakfast with his wife in the kitchen, reading the paper, when he says to his wife. "Hey, Ruthie, listen to this. Did you know that women use about thirty thousand words a day, whereas men only use fifteen thousand words?"
>
> "I think I know why," she replies. "Women have to say everything twice."
>
> Benjamin puts down the paper and says, "What?"

Shalom bayis is a *group* activity. One spouse may be the dominant player, but it takes two to merge the *shalom* to the *bayis*.

The smooth functioning of a family unit is no different than Shimon bar Yochai's warning about the man on the boat drilling a hole under his own feet, putting all the passengers at risk ("When the water enters, the whole boat sinks!").[8]

Therefore, regardless of conventional norms, each partner must see *shalom bayis* as an obligation directed not at the other, but at one's own self (*ein hadavar talui ela bi*, "it all depends on me").[9]

In short: take the initiative!

The *Chofetz Chaim*, commenting on why the Red Sea parted only *after* the Jews entered it, explains that Jews always need to make some effort and not rely only on miracles – this especially applies to finding a spouse, and working on *shalom bayis*.

> Yankie is walking with his *chaver* and says, "You know, ever since I got married I've gone through a miraculous transformation: I've become a walking economy."
>
> "What does that mean?" his friend replies.
>
> "Well, my hair line is in recession, my stomach is a victim of inflation, and both of these together are putting me into a deep depression!"

---

8.   *Vayikra Rabba* 4:6.
9.   *Avoda Zara* 17a.

One summer night Rabbi Nosson Tzvi Finkel, *rosh yeshiva* of Slobodka, was giving a *mussar shmuess* to several students. Night was coming, and his *rebbetzin* whispered in his ear, "What about their wives." Although he had not finished his *shmuess*, he immediately stopped and told them to go home right away, that it was not right to make their wives wait for them.[10]

Precious little is gained by demanding that "the other" live up to a "role" in *shalom bayis*; improving the home atmosphere is a joint obligation but each party has a *personal* responsibility that leaves no room for finger pointing.

Maintaining customary gender roles of responsibility, leaving no room for flexibility or compromise, or recognition of a new reality, is a sure-fire formula for marital tension.

Most people need to be respected, valued and appreciated.

If you take the initiative, your spouse will likely follow. If not, your frustration will build up to the hammer of hostility, nailing the coffin shut on any hopes of a blissful *shalom bayis*.[11]

> Beryl is complaining about his *shalom bayis* to the *rav*.
>
> "*Nu*, what's the problem, Beryl?" the *rav* sighs.
>
> "Well, I can't break my wife of the habit of staying up until five in the morning."
>
> "Five in the morning? What is she doing?"
>
> "Waiting for me to get home!"

In two important historic junctures, it was the Jewish woman who took the spiritual initiative.

The first occurred with the giving of the Torah, the "marriage ring" of the Jewish people, effective only after the women accepted it (Moshe is told to first instruct the *Beis Yaakov*, the women, and only then the *B'nei Yisroel*, the men, since it was futile to give Torah to the men unless the women underpinned it).

The second occasion was the building of the *Mishkan* (the Sanctuary). When Moshe launched his building campaign, the first offerings came from the women, who instinctively understood the communal advantages of having a centralized spiritual site.

---

10.   *Tenuas Hamussar*, vol. 3.
11.   *Yevamos* 62b; *Hilchos Ishus* 15:19, 20; *Kiddushin* 31, *Sota* 17a, *Avos d'Rabbi Nosson* 41.

Thus, nobility is preserved for the woman of the house ("The wise woman builds her house – and the foolish one tears it down with her own hands"),[12] and it is usually the wife's antennae that pick up the first signs of negative influences and threats to the household's harmony.

That's what happened to Sarah: To preserve her *shalom bayis*, she insisted that Yishmael be sent away.[13]

According to the Steipler Rav, *shalom bayis* starts by selecting and marrying someone with good *middos*, with "a good heart," who cares, has compassion, does *chesed* instinctively (the Steipler's great saying was that "the *shtender* never talks back, never gets sick, and never asks you to take the garbage out!").

In his essay on compassion in *Chorev*, Rav Shimshon Raphael Hirsch urges us to keep away from those who withhold their compassion. After describing a person who is "dead, without feeling,"[14] as being afflicted with *timtum halev*, "hardening of the heart," the Rambam warns that from such a spouse will come no mercy, no compassion, no sympathy. Or as the Yiddishists say: A blanket warms a person, but not a stone!

On one of Rabbi Paysach Krohn's tapes, he recalls how a woman called him once to inquire about a *yeshiva bochur* who was suggested for her daughter. He replied with only positive comments (fine boy, serious learner, good *middos*, etc).

She then asked, "But is he a *mechadesh*?" to which Rabbi Krohn replied, "How many *chiddushim* is he going to say when he's up at three in the morning with a crying baby?!"

Middos 'n manners equals *menschlichkeit*! As the saying goes: he may be in *Who's Who*, but what good is that if he doesn't know *What's What*!

> Pinchas, a young *yeshiva bochur*, has been sequestered in the *beis medrash* for years learning Torah and is totally unfamiliar with the ways of the world. When he reaches dating age, his rebbe urges him to start going out and meeting people. So Pinchas accepts an invitation to a yeshiva dinner. He walks along a fancy smorgasbord table and keeps putting his fingers in the dip. Finally, the caterer whispers to him, "Please

---

12.   *Mishlei* 14:1.
13.   *Bereishis* 21:10, 12.
14.   Rambam, *Hilchos Deios* 1:4.

don't put your fingers in the dip, it's not polite. That's what the crackers are for."

So Pinchas spends the rest of the evening putting his fingers in the crackers!

The town of Brisk was once in need of a *chazan*. The elders of the *kehilla* came to Rav Chaim Soloveitchik with a list of applications and attributes. Rav Chaim listened intently as they read them aloud. One candidate had a fear of Heaven. Another had exceptional *middos*. The next applicant was a noted *lamdan* (scholar). Another a warm personality. And so on…

All eyes were on Reb Chaim as he sat patiently, leaning forward, listening to the great praises of worthy candidates. Finally, he leaned back, a look of frustration on his face. "Did anybody inquire from these gentlemen if they knew how to sing?!"

A man once came to Rabbi Avraham Yeshaya Karelitz to tell him that his daughter was engaged.

After singing the praises of the boy (good learner, good family, etc.), the *Chazon Ish*, as related by Rabbi Shlomo Lorincz in his memoirs *In Their Shadow*, patiently said, "But did you ask if he would make a good husband? If that quality is lacking, it is not a good match, no matter how many other positive qualities he possesses!"

Arrogance and marriage are a recipe for disaster.

According to the *Yalkut Shimoni*, an aggadic compilation on the Torah, the sins of Nadav and Avihu, the sons of Aaron who were "consumed by a fire from above," resulted from their arrogant assumption that "Our paternal uncle is the king, our maternal uncle is the *nasi* [prince], our father is the *kohen gadol* [high priest], and we are the vice-kohens. What woman is suitable for us?"[15]

> Parents of a girl are interviewing a potential *shidduch* and are impressed with his *middos* but worried about the boy's lack of earning potential. The boy tries to reassure them, "*Zorg zich nisht*, don't worry. I promise I'll keep your daughter in the style and manner she's been accustomed to."
>
> "How?" asks the father.
>
> "By moving in with you!"

---

15. *Vayikra* 9:22–24.

Rav Moshe of Kobrin, the Slonimer Rebbe, differentiated between *acts* of *chesed* and a *personality* of *chesed*, the latter defined by our Sages as "one who runs" to be kind to others ("A day that a Jew does not do a kindness is not considered a day in his life!").[16]

This personality of *chesed* was at the core of Avraham's character, as defined by the Midrash: "God said to Job, 'You do not reach half of Avraham's level. You sit in your house and wait for guests; Avraham would run out [even on the third day after his circumcision at the age of ninety-nine] searching for them.'"[17]

For thousands of years all rabbinic texts on *shalom bayis* refer back to *Parshas Chayei Sarah*, the "*parsha* of *shidduchim*,"[18] and the three[19] marriage qualities that Eliezer, Avraham's servant, saw in Rivka at the well: hospitality to strangers, generosity (*chesed*), and compassion (giving the camels water to drink).[20]

These three *middos* (personality traits)[21] were so important to Jewish genealogy that our Sages say their absence indicates some non-Jewish (Gibeonite)

---

16.   *Nesivos Shalom*, vol. 1.

17.   *Avos d'Rabbi Nosson*.

18.   During the Middle Ages there was literally a "marriage marketplace." From a mid-seventeenth-century *sefer*: "He who had a son or a daughter to marry journeyed to the fair [held at Lemberg and Lublin] and there made a match, for everyone found his like and his suit." Thousands of matches were made as a result of these fairs. In Medieval Europe, the most illustrious *shadchan* was the Maharil. Shadchan fees ranged from 1 to 2 percent of the dowry, paid by both sides. There was no rent (the new couple lived in the bride's family home for a few years), and the bride's father (not the community) paid for his son-in-law's continued Torah learning for at least a year.

19.   The number "three" is not accidental. It has religious significance. There are three partners in a marriage (man, woman, God); the Torah, paralleling three forefathers (Avraham, Yitzchak, Yaakov) is described by three adjectives ("the Torah of truth, kindness, life"); all matters relating to Torah appear in three-somes (*Talmud Bavli*, *Shabbat* 88a): "Blessed be God who gave the three-part Torah (Torah, Prophets, Holy Writings) to the three-fold nation (Priests, Levites, Israelites) in the third month (*Sivan*) by means of the three (Moshe, Aaron and Miriam)." And how many "legs" does the world stand on? Three! "On Torah study, on the service of God, on kind deeds" (*Pirkei Avos* 1:2).

20.   *Bereishis* 24:12.

21.   The literal meaning of *midda* is "measure." This refers to the measure of a person's personality or character.

background, and the *Shulchan Aruch* even goes so far as to warn, "It is improper to marry one who lacks these distinguishing characteristics."[22]

These internal qualities inspired the Tehillim lyrics, "*Kol kevuda bas Melech penima* (The whole glory of the daughter of the King is within)."[23]

The medieval Torah scholar Me'iri elaborated: "Even though there are many things that one has to search for in selecting a mate in terms of family, it is more important to look for character and principled conduct."

> After their guests leave from a Shabbas meal, Debbie turns to her husband: "You have such bad manners! I'm so embarrassed! Whenever we have people over you never listen when they talk to you! You get this stupid faraway look in your eyes and your mind wanders off! You have to improve your ways! Promise me you'll do that!"
>
> He turns to her and says, "Sorry, honey. What were you saying?"

In the olden days, the local water well was the place to make a *shidduch*.[24] Moshe, Yitzchak and Yaakov meet their brides Tzippora, Rivka and Rachel near wells (maybe this is where the expression *well, well, well* comes from?).

Why a well? Apart from the obvious (that's where the water is), Jewish mystics see the Hebrew term for well (*be'er*) as an acronym of the *Tehillim* verse "*beyadcha afkid ruchi* (in Your hands I deposit my soul)."[25]

The first spontaneous prayer in the Torah comes from Eliezer as he asks for Divine guidance before setting out to find the ideal wife for Yitzchak. Eliezer's is one of only three prayers in the Torah that is answered immediately after being recited (the other two who are similarly blessed are Moshe and Shlomo Hamelech).

---

22. It is a Sephardi *minhag* to read the story of Eliezer's search for a bride on the Shabbas of the wedding, in addition to the regular Torah portion. Rabbeinu Bachya explains why: "To caution the community not to marry for beauty or for money, and to stay close to their families. One who marries an unworthy person for good looks or money will have children who are unworthy – and the money will not last!"
23. *Tehillim* 45:14.
24. *Shemos Rabba* 1:32; *Bereishis* 24:62; 29:2; *Shemos* 2:15.
25. *Tehillim* 31:6.

Ironically, everyone's name is mentioned in this Torah portion (*Chayei Sara*) – Avraham (thirty-seven times), Sarah (nine times), Efron (nine times), Yitzchak (thirteen times), Rivka (twelve times), Besuel (four times), Lavan (three times) – and yet the name of the star of the saga, Eliezer, the *shadchan* himself, is not mentioned once (perhaps a hint that the *shadchan* should always stay in the background?).

> "Nu," the *shadchan* asks the boy who has just gotten engaged the day before, "how was dinner there last night? Aren't they a fine, high-class family? Did you notice all the the pure sterling silverware?"
>
> "Yes," the young man agrees, but with no enthusiasm. "Perhaps they borrowed all that expensive silverware just to impress me?"
>
> "Borrowed it?" shouts the *shadchan*. "Are you crazy! Who in their right mind would lend expensive silver to those *ganavim* [crooks]?"

How does one judge a man's character?

By his "walk, dress and greeting [and by the way he handles] business, wine and conversation," and through his "portion, potion and passion."[26]

As soon as Rivka notices her future husband approaching she covers herself with a veil.[27]

From this act of bashfulness and modesty, we add a fourth quality to a good marriage: *tznius* (this applies not only to the wife; husbands need to be reserved as well, in body language, speech, clothes, etc.).

Meanwhile, Jewish mystics believe that, since the first *shidduch* in history (Adam and Eve, the ultimate "Made-to-Order" marriage as God Himself both

---

26. *Avos d'Rabbi Nosson* 31; Ilai, *Eruvin* 65b.
27. This led to the custom of *bedeken*, when, prior to the *chuppa* the *chasan* lifts the veil of the *kalla* to "check" it's the right girl. This is derived from Yaakov's father-in-law substituting Leah for Rachel at his marriage. As he lowers the veil he says, "Our sister, may you be the mother of thousands of ten thousands," words which were first said to Rivka by her mother and brother when she left home to marry Yitzchak (*Bereishis* 24:60, 65).

creates and presents the bride to the groom),[28] "it is the way of man to search for woman."[29] Why? He is spiritually searching for his own lost side (rib).[30]

The first step in finding the right spouse requires an honest soul-searching *cheshbon hanefesh* (literally, an accounting of the soul; call it the *Shalom Bayis Reality Check!*).

You need to know who *you* are, what *your* strengths and needs are.

It's not enough to find "Mr. Right," you need to find "Mr. Right for me!" – and remember: each of you is still a work in progress, so common goals, dreams, aspirations and interests, as well as tolerance, patience and fortitude are just as important for marital compatibility as physical attraction and enjoying each other's company.

> The girl was being interviewed by a *shadchan*.
>
> "What type of boy are you looking for?" he asked.
>
> "All I want in a husband is a man who is learned, kind, good-looking. Surely that's not too much to expect from a multi-millionaire?"

---

28. Shmuly sees a pretty girl at a bar mitzva, walks by her and says, "Do you believe in love at first sight – or would you like me to walk by again?" The Midrash and the *Zohar* say that God "fell in love" with the Jewish people and that it was this love at first sight that motivated God to create the world (*Bereishis Rabba* 8:7; *Zohar Chadash* 121c). There are four more explicit examples of love at first sight in the Torah. The first is Rivka for Yitzchak (*Bereishis* 24:64–65), Yaakov for Rachel – the Torah's prototypical example of romantic love (*Bereishis* 29), David for Avigayil (*I Shmuel* 25), and David for Batsheva (*II Shmuel* 12). Based on Rivka's reaction when she saw Yitzchak (she fell off her camel), the *Netziv, rosh yeshiva* of Volozhin, says that a couple's first meeting has a great impact (*Ha'amek Davar, Bereishis* 24:67). The word *ahava* appears only once in Avraham's life, and refers to his relationship to his son ("Take your son, your only one, whom you love [*asher ahavta*], Yitzchak" to the *akeida*). In Yitzchak's life, it appears often, in relationship to his wife Rivka (*vaye'ehaveha*), his sons (Yitzchak loved Eisav; Rivka loves [*oheves*] Yaakov), even to his taste in food (Yitzchak asks Eisav to bring him savory food *ka'asher ahavti*, "the way I love"). Surely the longest search for a family was Yaakov's. According to the Midrash, Yaakov was sixty-three when he was sent by his parents to find a wife in Charan. He "tarried" for fourteen years in the yeshiva world (learning with Shem and Ever), and arrived in Charan at seventy-seven. He then took another fourteen years before he finally managed to get married – to two sisters (Leah and Rachel).
29. *Kiddushin* 2b.
30. *Bereishis Rabba* 17:6.

Rav Shlomo Ephraim ben Aaron Luntschitz, the sixteenth-century rabbi best known for his Torah commentary *Kli Yakar*, commenting on the Talmud's statement "A bride who has beautiful eyes need not be examined any further,"[31] explains that "beautiful eyes" implies that she deals with others generously, and not with a "miserly eye."

Jews who excel in generosity, he adds, will excel in other positive areas as well.

"As water reflects a face with a face," noted Shlomo Hamelech, "in this way the heart of one person reflects the heart of another person."[32]

In other words, if you show heartfelt appreciation of all your spouse's *maalos* (good attributes), and display heartfelt warmth and concern, the same appreciation, warmth and concern will surely "boomerang" back to you.

> Abie bumps into his friend Sam as he comes out of a jewelry store in Boro Park carrying a small gift-wrapped box.
>
> "*Nu*, Abe. What did you buy today?"
>
> "Well, it's my Rifka's birthday tomorrow and when I asked her this morning what she wanted she said, in her usual humility, 'Oh, I don't know, dear, just give me something with a lot of diamonds in it.'"
>
> "So what did you get her?"
>
> "I bought her a pack of cards!"

If the family unit was a government, the wife's *tafkid* (function) would be the role of interior minister, with her husband (who receives blessings "only in the merit of his wife!")[33] playing the role of foreign minister.

Of course, spending most of his time with the general public does not absolve the husband of interior responsibility; this includes running off to Torah *shiurim* at times when the mother needs a visible and involved father at home. Emotional isolation is a slow eradicator of *shalom bayis*.

If a wife doesn't want her husband to go to night *seder*, Rav Moshe Aharon Stern, *mashgiach* in Kamenitz and grandson of the famed *tzadik* Reb Yaakov Yosef Herman, writes, "He should not begin the night *chavrusa*, because otherwise the

---

31. *Taanis* 24a.

32. *Mishlei* 27:19.

33. *Bava Metzia* 59a.

wife will suffer from loneliness…. Today many girls have learned to appreciate learning in Beis Yaakov, but nevertheless, situations can arise where a wife cannot handle such an arrangement. In such cases one must not forge ahead [in Torah learning] without her approval."

Before he would sit down to learn Torah, Rav Yisroel Yitzchak Zilberman would tell his wife, "Henneh, if you want anything tell me now, because after I start learning I won't stop!"

The *Chazon Ish* once ordered a young man in *kollel* to go home, "help your wife feed the children and put them to sleep, and then return to your studies." Rav Moshe Feinstein ruled that if your wife feels pressured, it's better to stay home and help her make sandwiches in the morning and take the children to the school bus than to hurry off to shul.

Rabbi Yosef Epstein, one of the *rabbonim* who escaped Europe with the Mirrer Yeshiva through Shanghai, ruled that if a husband's Torah learning deprives his wife of time that she needs from him, he must reduce the amount of time spent learning and ease his wife's discomfort.

Rav Yosef defined this as a *middos* improvement (*shleimus*, "self-perfection") which raises the "level of holiness" in the home.[34] When asked if the husband was guility of *bitul Torah*, "nullifying Torah learning," Rav Yosef answered *No*, and then pointed out the myriad *shalom bayis* mitzvos he was performing instead: pleasing his wife, helping her with home duties, pursuing peace, humility, etc.

In honor of both their wives and Shabbas, the Gemora records that our great sages were accustomed to contribute personally to the Shabbas preparations in their households: Rabbi Abbahu fanned the fire, Rav Safra prepared meat, Rava salted fish, Rav Huna lit the lantern, Rav Pappa prepared candle wicks, Rav Chisda chopped beets, Rabba and Rav Yosef split wood for the fire, and Rav Nachman carried packages.[35]

---

34. *Sefer Mitzvos Habayis.*
35. *Shabbas* 119a.

Wanting to give his four-year-old daughter a sense of what marriage is all about, Yankele takes out his wedding album and explains the entire service to her. Once finished, his daughter looks up and asks, "Oh, now I get it, Tatte. That's when Mommy came to work for us, right?"[36]

The Talmud asks why five men are called up to the Torah on *yom tov* and not seven, as on Shabbas.[37] The answer? The men come later to *shul*. So? Rashi explains that this is because the *yom tov* meal is being prepared at home.

This prompted Rav Yaakov Emden, son of the Chacham Tzvi and prolific halachic author (*Sheeilas Yaavetz*), to ask, "But the cooking is done by women, so why should this make men come late to shul?"

The *Yaavetz* answers that when the women are cooking for *yom tov*, their husbands should be helping take care of the house and the children.

In fact, Jewish law often establishes priorities when there are conflicting Torah demands upon an individual.

When a man marries, he is subjugating himself to the Torah by paying attention to his wife and providing for her needs ("*Ana eflach v'okir...va'afarnes* [I shall work and honor...and support]"), both being legal obligations in his *kesuba*, a legally binding contract that obligates a husband to support his wife financially.

After Rabbi Elchanan Wasserman refused to accept any pay from his yeshiva, he received a letter from the Rav of Vilna, Chaim Ozer Grodzinski, his brother-in-law, chastising him for not providing his family with their minimal needs.

"You may be a *tzadik* for yourself," Rav Chaim Ozer writes, "and be content with less than the minimum, as you indeed do, but you have no right to do so with regard to your wife and children, especially since your wife is the daughter of Rabbi Meir Atlas, the *av beis din* of Shavli. When you married her you knew that she had never lacked for anything in her father's house. Her father made

---

36.   Being a "mother of Israel" is an honor (God could not be everywhere, goes the Yiddish proverb, so He created mothers). When the Ark of the Covenant was returned to Israel from Phillistine captivity, King David danced in front of it. His wife, Michal, objected to her husband's behavior. She felt it was inappropriate for the king of Israel to dance wildly in the presence of the "women and maids (*imahos, amahos*)." Because she denigrated the institution of motherhood, she was punished, and didn't have a child until the day she died (*II Shmuel* 6:16–20, 23).

37.   *Megilla* 23a.

an honorable living as befits the rabbi of a large community. You took it upon yourself in the *kesuba* to provide for all her needs. This obligation is a duty that cannot be evaded.... Please excuse me for having deemed it necessary to point out this matter to you."

The rabbis of the Talmud preferred the Jew "flay carcasses in the marketplace" and earn an honest living rather than say, "A man of my station is too important to do such work!"[38]

Recognizing that full-time learning immediately after the *chuppa* "limits and curbs [one's ability to earn a livelihood] and slightly reduces the ability to obtain one's material needs...which is felt on a daily basis," the Lubavitcher Rebbe urged husbands to make sure their wife is in "full-fledged joyous agreement" with this arrangement before getting married.[39]

The Vilna Gaon cautions that one should never assume that Torah automatically improves someone. As an analogy, noting that the Jew needs Torah just as the earth needs moisture, he reminds us that watering a garden can go either way, creating beautiful flowers – or nasty weeds!

> The father was worried about the *middos* of the boy his daughter was engaged to, and started to inquire about his work ethic and ability to support a new family. "So tell me," the father asks one night, "what will your yearly income be?"
>
> "Around forty-five thousand."
>
> "Well, that's not too bad, especially when you add my daughter's forty thousand income."
>
> "I already did!"

"The main purpose of man's creation in this world," according to the Baal Shem Tov, who was quoting Rav Saadia Gaon, "is to break his bad character traits!"

The Torah's influence depends on the preexisting personality (*middos*) of an individual.

If the man is "good," Torah will make his goodness better and he will be an exemplary husband; if he is already inclined to bad behavior, marriage could make those bad traits even worse.

A *"frum"* person who lacks *derech eretz* within marriage is a practitioner of

---

38. *Pesachim* 113a; *Shulchan Aruch, Even Ha'ezer* 69–74.
39. *Likkutei Sichos*, vol. 34.

hypocrisy, a contradiction to the pursuit of a polite, thoughtful and civil *shalom bayis*.

Commenting on the third chapter of *Pirkei Avos* ("If one doesn't have *derech eretz*, one doesn't have Torah"), Rav Eliyahu Eliezer Dessler, the influential *mashgiach ruchani* of Ponovezh Yeshiva, quotes Rav Yonah's claim that God's Presence cannot rest upon anybody with bad *middos* – even if they have lots of Torah learning.[40]

Next time you go to a *bris*, note the order of blessings: the community wants the boy (*first*) to grow up to achieve "Torah" (and *only then* go on to) "marriage and good deeds."

> "My husband gambles," the wife confides to her friend. "Just last week he went to Las Vegas in a $50,000 car and returned a few days later in a $100,000 vehicle."
>
> "Wow! He won that much money? He must really know how to gamble."
>
> "Well, not exactly. He went in our car but had to come back by bus!"

Rav Avrohom Blumenkrantz, a young confidant of Rav Moshe Feinstein and prominent *posek* on the laws of Pesach, once told me that if on the way home a husband gave money to a beggar on the street, and then later denied his wife's request for a new dress, his mitzva of *tzedaka* was nullified.

This obligation, writes Rav Aharon Moshe Stern, "is greater than for anyone else. There are people who behave very charitably outside their homes, but if their wives are asked they'd say their husbands are far from charitable. The word *chesed* has two meanings: kindness and disgrace. The person who is charitable outside but not at home fulfills both meanings. He is kind outside and a disgrace inside!"

This attitude of "home first" comes from Rav Chaim Vital.

In his sefer *Shaarei Kedusha*, the famed sixteenth-century kabbalist claims that, when a man is summoned to the High Court, God will disregard a lifetime of *chesed* – unless he had acted with kindness towards his wife. Rav Chaim adds that when one does constant mitzvos with strangers, but mistreats or neglects anyone in the immediate family, the punishment vastly outweighs any rewards for those "external" kind deeds.

---

40. E.E. Dessler, *Michtav Me'Eliyahu*, vol. 4.

Rav Shmuel Salant would climb up to the roof of his house to help his wife hang the laundry. When she complained, "It's not fitting for the *rav* of Yerushalayim to hang laundry," he replied he had no say in it. "It's a mitzva!"

Rav Eliyahu Dov Laizerovitch, *rosh yeshiva* of Kelm, was totally involved in running the yeshiva from early morning to late at night. Nevertheless, he would get up earlier than his wife (who baked bread for a living) to stoke the oven to allow her to sleep longer.

A student once asked Rav Shlomo Zalman Auerbach while he was sitting in Rav Avigdor Nebenzahl's succa in Jerusalem, how much a husband should spend on clothing for his wife in order to fulfill the mitzva of making her happy on *yom tov*.

A smiling Rebbetzin Auerbach, trying to impress that it's the thought that counts, replied that one year her husband bought her a simple vegetable peeler – and she had never been happier!

> Moishie decides he has to be more helpful around the house so he asks his wife if there's anything she needs from the store.
>
> "Yes, eggs," she replies.
>
> So he goes to the store and asks the salesgirl, "How much are these eggs?"
>
> "Sixty cents for the small, seventy cents for the medium, ninety cents for the large, and thirty cents for the cracked ones."
>
> "OK. Crack me a dozen of the large ones."

The first chapter in *Pirkei Avos* gives some good marriage advice: always judge others favorably, always give them the benefit of the doubt! This will create a positive atmosphere in the home. And more! Always show the utmost appreciation (*hakaras hatov*) to your partner.

A home lacking gratitude is fundamentally an empty shell. An ungrateful spouse is a serious impediment to marital harmony.

The logic behind *hakaras hatov* is to sharpen your sensitivities towards others.

When the Torah opens its book of *Shemos* with the statement "A new king arose over Egypt who did not know Yosef," it immediately traces the future problems of the Jews to a king's extraordinary lack of appreciation.

Yosef had saved the Egyptian people from an oppressive famine. The new ruler lacked a basic human quality: *hakaras hatov*.[41]

Rav Yitzchak Hutner, the "Warsaw Illui" who became the innovative *rosh yeshiva* of Chaim Berlin, would often point out that the Hebrew word *hodaʾa* could mean either "admitting" or "giving thanks." In order to say *Thank you* to another person, you must admit that you are less than perfect.

Thus the literal translation of the term in the thanksgiving *bracha* in the *Shemoneh Esrei* (*Modim anachnu lach*) is not "We thank You" but "We admit to You."

Never become demanding, was Rav Dessler's advice to young married couples. "Demands create negative feelings. Always be giving. This, as a rule, leads to *shalom bayis*."

In fact, Rabbi David ben Yosef Avudraham, the Spanish author of one of the most popular works on *tefilla*, points out that one can appoint an agent (the *shaliach tzibur*) for all the blessings in the *Shemoneh Esrei* ("Heal us," "Bless us," etc.) except for one, which must be said personally, and that is "Thank You."

This humility is the bedrock of *shalom bayis*.

On his return from *shul* Friday nights, Rabbi Simcha Zissel Ziv would not enter his home immediately, but would pause by the door and gaze at the set table for Shabbas and the pleasant food his wife had prepared.

He did this to feel grateful every week for all that she did for him.[42]

Rav Chaim Leib Shmuelevitz of Mir, a *mussar* master, commenting on *shalom bayis*, pointed to the Torah episode of the three angels visiting Avraham.

---

41.   The Midrash traces the Jewish attitude of being thankful (our first words in the morning are *Modeh ani lefanecha*, thanking God for allowing us to wake up) to Leah. Leah was convinced that Yaakov would raise twelve tribes, with each of his four wives bearing him three children. Thus, when she gave birth to her fourth son (Yehuda), she felt God had given her more than she deserved, and said, "This time I will give thanks [*odeh*] to God" (*Bereishis* 29:35), thus incorporating the attribute of giving thanks into the DNA of her descendants. The first time Jews are referred to as *Yehudim* is in *Megillas Esther* (the first *mitzva miʾdʾrabbanan* instituted by the rabbis) because by then the Jewish people consisted only of survivors from Yehuda (Judea).

42.   *Tenuas Hamussar*, vol. 2.

The guests inquire of their host, "*Ayeh Sarah ishtecha* (Where is Sarah)?"

Rashi explains that this is not idle chatter but has a purpose (*k'dei l'chabeva al baala*, in order to endear her to her husband). The angels know already that Sarah is in the tent; by asking where she is they highlight her modesty and thus encourage Avraham, at age ninety-nine, to appreciate his ninety-eight-year-old wife, to ensure that, even after a lengthy marriage, she is further endeared to him.[43]

Rav Aharon Moshe Stern recalls escorting Rav Shlomo Zalman Auerbach home after *davening*. "The weather was stormy and his *peyos* whipped around untidily in the wind. Before entering his home he tidied his beard and explained to me, 'A wife shouldn't have to see her husband disheveled. When a man walks into his home, he should look neat and pleasant.' I was astonished, because he'd been married about fifty years and still felt the need to tidy himself to please his wife."

> Beryl is celebrating his fortieth wedding anniversary and his best friend asks him, "*Nu*, what have you have learned from all these wonderful years with your wife?"
>
> "Well," Beryl replies, "I've learned that marriage is the best teacher of all. It teaches you loyalty, forbearance, meekness, self-restraint, forgiveness – and a great many other qualities you wouldn't have needed if you'd stayed single."

Rabbi Boruch Ber Leibowitz, *rosh yeshiva* of Kaminetz, was in America on a fund-raising trip and knocked on the door of a wealthy Jew. The man immediately recognized the *rosh yeshiva* and became embarrassed because his wife was listening to secular music on the radio.

He excused himself for a moment and went to his wife and demanded that she immediately turn off the radio. He then returned to the *rosh yeshiva* and invited Rav Boruch Ber in. But instead the *rosh yeshiva* asked him to step outside for a moment so he could talk to him.

The husband was very nervous, expecting to be rebuked for listening to popular music.

Instead, the *rosh yeshiva* said, "Your wife was having *hano'a* [enjoyment] from listening to that music. Go inside, apologize for making her turn it off, beg her to forgive you, put the music back on, and then I'll come inside."

---

43. Rashi, *Bereishis* 18:9.

Yehuda Loew ben Bezalel, the Maharal of Prague, was convinced that discord is actually dominant in the world, and it is up to people to promote *shalom*.[44]

This is why many of the mitzvos are expressed in terms of reacting *to* or *after* an event (*ki yifga, ki yikarei*, etc.), with the exception of peace, which the Torah demands must be "pursued," not after, but *before*, any discord.[45]

It is inevitable: within each marriage come times of adjustment. Compatibility is not constant. Don't be scared to take the first step. Insecurity in the status quo can lead to a quick deterioration in the home.

As we all know, no individual is perfect, all are flawed. Even God, perfect in all ways, shows what we would call "anger" and "jealousy." Thus, when trying to adjust, never accentuate the negative, always magnify the positives in your spouse.

"What's the ultimate virtue?" asks Solomon ibn Gabriel. He answers, "Patience with the vices of others!"

> Moishie and his wife Suri are meeting with their *rav*.
>
> "How can I help you?" the rabbi asks.
>
> "It's my wife, Rabbi," Moishie begins, "she's always very negative."
>
> "That's not true," interjects Suri, "I've now become an optimist!"
>
> "That's great!" says the *rav*, "but tell me, Suri, how come you look so down and worried?"
>
> "What! You think it's easy being an optimist?!"

In the olden days, it was the bride who wore an olive wreath at the *chuppa*, symbolic of the "peace" and "goodwill" that she – and the olive branch – represented.

"Extending an olive branch" soon became a worldwide metaphor for the hope of peace.[46]

Its genesis as a universal symbol of peace comes from the image of a white dove returning to Noah with an olive leaf in its beak, a sign from God that He had taken mercy on humanity and caused the flood waters to recede.

---

44. Maharal, *Nesiv Hashalom* 2.
45. *Vayikra Rabba* 25.
46. The appearance of a rainbow also became a sign of relief. Ancient warriors would turn their bows (symbolic of a rainbow) towards themselves to indicate that they were laying down their arms and ending hostilities.

The dove seeks *mano'ach*, "a peaceful resting place," from which we get the word *menucha*, "rest" (literally, the calm after the storm!), now associated with the day of Shabbas.

In the Torah, *shemen* (oil) always refers exclusively to olive oil.[47]

Why the olive? Some Torah scholars point out that olive trees take a long time to bear fruit; thus too with peace. It needs time to mature, and its longevity is its own reward.

In rabbinic texts the olive was synonymous with wisdom and peace. Israel's optimistic coat of arms today is a menora flanked by two olive branches. The eagle on the Great Seal of the United States shows an olive branch grasped in its right talon, and the seal of the United Nations features olive branches.

Olive trees can live for hundreds of years, and produce fruit for centuries. Olive was the Torah's preferred choice of oil because, being free of sediment, it burns with a bright light (*shalom*) – and with little smoke (discord) to cloud the picture.

> Shmuly is concerned that his wife needs glasses so he encourages her to go to an eye doctor. She hasn't been for seven years and her vision is getting blurry. When she arrives the receptionist gives her a form to fill out.
>
> In response to the question "Reason for visiting doctor," she writes, "Long time no see!"

---

47.   *Yalkut Shimoni* 1:378.

One Step Closer

Finding one's *shidduch* is a process. For some the process goes, *Baruch Hashem*, quickly, while for others it takes longer. For example, in the late 1940s there was an older *bochur* in 770 who was having difficulty finding a *shidduch*. Why? Whenever a name was proposed to him, he would send in a note to the Frierdiker Rebbe asking if he should proceed with the *shidduch*. And each time. the Rebbe said no. This happened five or six times over the course of a few months.

The *bochur* figured out on his own that since the Rebbe was rejecting all the offers, it must mean that he was not destined to marry; he should spend his life sitting and learning Torah. He therefore began turning down all further offers on his own, without consulting the Rebbe. After a while, the Rebbe himself inquired as to why no more offers from this young man were being proposed. The *bochur* described his interpretation of the Rebbe's answers.

The Frierdiker Rebbe replied with a story. The Berditchiver Rav had a son named Reb Meir who died young, leaving behind several young children, whom the Berditchiver raised in his home. When the time came to marry off the oldest, the Berditchiver told all the *shadchanim* to come forward with suggestions, announcing that he would reward each one whether or not the *shidduch* was successful. The offers poured in and the Berditchiver refused them all but paid regardless. This happened time and time again. At a certain point the *shadchanim* spoke among themselves and decided to stop sending in names so that they would not waste the *rav*'s money.

When the Berditchiver noticed that no new names were forthcoming, he asked the *shadchanim* what was going on. They explained that if he would pay for only the *shidduch* that was successful, they would continue to come forward with suggestions. But to take all of the *rav*'s money, just for making suggestions? How could they do such a thing?

The Berditchiver explained that every time a new name is suggested, we take one step closer to the *bashert*.

Before a person is born, it is decided who will be his or her *bashert*. There are many *shadchanim* in *Shamayim* and each one proposes an idea. Maybe Gittel is good for him – no, I think Shprintza – or how about Baila...until the *Aibishter* decides on one. But we have to go through all the *malachim*'s ideas until we reach the right one. When a *shidduch* is about to happen and at the last minute it falls through, it is because there were two strong contenders and the *Aibishter* saw strong *maalos* in both and at the last minute came to a conclusion.

So, the Frierdiker Rebbe continued saying to this *bochur*, each time that the Berditchiver refused a *shidduch*, he knew he was coming closer to the correct one, and he was willing to pay for this kind of progress.

Obviously, the *bochur* went back to reporting all offers to the Rebbe, and asking his advice. A few weeks later the proper name came up, the Rebbe indicated that it was a good idea, and the young man soon became a *chasan*. Today, he has many grandchildren and great-grandchildren, *baruch Hashem*. Parents should not get disillusioned and depressed if the process is longer for their child, and they certainly should not allow themselves to think that something is wrong with their child; most importantly, they should not transmit such an unhelpful attitude to their child, whether in words or in facial expressions or even in sighs. Keep trying, remain positive, and the time will come.

– Rabbi Leibel Groner, secretary to the Lubavitcher Rebbe

The Sofer and His Wife

The *Shulchan Aruch* rules that "It is forbidden for a *sofer* (a ritual scribe) to interrupt his work while writing the name of Hashem. Even if the king of the Jewish people greets him, he may not answer until he finishes the name."[48]

Still, a story is told about a *talmid chacham* who was in the middle of writing Hashem's name when his wife, carrying heavy shopping bags, knocked on the door. Rather than waiting the extra minute to finish the name, the *sofer* put down his quill and ran to open the door. He reasoned that if Hashem allowed His name to be erased for the sake of *shalom bayis*, then he could certainly interrupt his writing for the sake of *shalom bayis!*[49]

---

48. *Yoreh Deah* 276:3.
49. The *sofer* relied on the *psak* of Reb Shabtai Hakohen, the *Shach*, that while it is forbidden to interrupt the writing of God's name, after the fact, his work is still kosher.

Rav Eliezer Shach Helps Out

A young yeshiva man used to *daven k'vasikin* (at dawn) on *Shabbas* mornings. During the summertime, the *minyan* ended rather early in the morning, so he used to stay in *shul* a while longer to learn.

One *Shabbas* morning the man was so tired that he fell asleep over his Gemora and did not awaken until 11:00 a.m. Shocked by how long he had slept and worried about what his wife might be thinking, he started to run home. On his way, he met Rav Shach, who asked him, "What is the rush? Have you finished your *seuda* so quickly that you are rushing to the *beis medrash* to learn?"

"Not really," replied the young man. "I fell asleep over my Gemora and am now rushing home to make Kiddush."

"Do you mean to say that your wife has been waiting all this time, not knowing what happened to you? Let me escort you home and I will explain what happened. Perhaps she will have an easier time accepting it from me…"

Rav Shimshon Raphael Hirsch on Choosing a Wife

When you choose a wife, remember that she is to be your companion in life, in building up your home, in the performance of your life task, and choose accordingly. It should not be wealth or physical beauty or brilliance of mind that makes you decide whom to marry. Rather, look for richness of heart, beauty of character, and good sense and intelligence. If, in the end, you require money, and your wife's family freely offers it to you, you may take it; but woe to you and your future household if you are guided only by considerations of money.

Study well the character of your future wife; but since character is first revealed by contact with real life, and since the girl usually first comes into contact with real life only with marriage, look well at her family. If you see a family in which disputes and quarreling are rife, in which insolence and evil talk are common, in which you behold hard-heartedness, hate and uncharitableness, do not attach yourself to it. According to the view of our Sages, even the Jewish descent of such a family is considered doubtful.

That you should keep aloof from all marriages forbidden by Torah and the Rabbis goes without saying. Our Sages recommend that one should always look for the daughter of a learned man, of a man in whom the public has shown its confidence by entrusting him with communal office – above all, of a man whose daughter can be expected to have learned practical wisdom from the example of her father.

– Rav Shimshon Raphael Hirsch,
in the discussion of marriage laws in his book *Chorev*

Don't Forget to Cover the *Challos*!

One Friday night the *Chofetz Chaim* visited the home of a man who berated his wife for not remembering to cover the *challos* before the recitation of Kiddush, causing her to leave the table in tears. The *Chofetz Chaim*, in addressing this uncomfortable situation, was able to use his wisdom to give the intemperate husband a sense of perspective. Drawing from sources in Jewish law, he pointed out to the man that one reason that we cover the *challos* is to shield them from the "embarrassment" of not receiving the first *bracha* of the meal. Accordingly, asked the *Chofetz Chaim*, how could Kiddush be recited when the man's own wife had been embarrassed? The man immediately understood the error of his ways and begged his wife for forgiveness.

The Satmar Rav on the Splitting of the Red Sea

What does Rabbi Yochanan mean when he states, "*V'kasheh l'zavgan k'kriyas yam suf*," that matching couples is "as difficult as splitting the Red Sea"?[50]

The Satmar Rav finds an answer in Tehillim, specifically the verse "*L'gozer yam suf li'gzarim*," that the Red Sea was split into "multiple components."[51]

One Midrash says the Sea was split into twelve paths, one for each of the twelve tribes; another Midrash says it split into six hundred thousand paths, one for each family. The question is obvious: why not just one path for all?

Each person, the Satmar Rav explains, has a different personality trait, different background, different mission in life. Splitting the Sea into six hundred thousand "private" paths implies that each Jew has a singular destiny, a unique spiritual capacity.

Similarly with marriage. Matching two people with their own personalities and unique purposes in life into *zivugin* (couples) that are, and stay, compatible – while successfully pursuing and promoting a common mission – is miraculous. Finding two that are compatible is a near impossibility, a task only God, the ultimate *Shadchan*, is capable of.[52]

---

50. *Pesachim* 118b; *Sota* 2a; *Sanhedrin* 22a.
51. *Tehillim* 136:13.
52. Perhaps a lesson from the Red Sea, in the context of getting married, is the fact that God tells Moses not to waste his time praying but to be more proactive in his situation. This led Nachshon ben Aminadav to take a chance, based solely on faith, and step out into the raging waters. In other words, if you're looking for a *shidduch*, don't be passive about it and rely solely on a match from Heaven. You too must "step out" as often as possible and perhaps rely less on what looks great on paper. Remember: "on paper," Moses would never have married the daughter of a priest.

Rav Moshe Shmuel Shapira on How to Respect One's Wife

The *rosh yeshiva* of Be'er Yaakov, Rav Moshe Shmuel Shapira, always treated his wife with the greatest respect. On Shabbas, she would sit at the opposite end of the table. Whenever he would make *Hamotzi*, he would get up himself to bring the *challa* to his *rebbetzin*, and always with the same shining smile. He explained once to his students that he didn't want to simply pass her the piece since she would feel more comfortable getting it from him directly.

Once, the *rav* and the *rebbetzin* were slated to travel to a wedding. When the student who was giving them a ride arrived, he found the *rosh yeshiva* (who was already in his seventies) ready and waiting. The *rebbetzin* apologized for the delay and asked if it was possible for the *rosh yeshiva* to wait a few minutes until she was ready. The *rosh yeshiva* responded, "*Rebbetzin!* As long as you are not yet ready, we aren't waiting because we are ready to go and you are delaying us. Quite the contrary! Until you are ready, the time to go has not yet arrived!"

One time, a close disciple, Rav Yisroel Meir Kohen Arzi, was with the *rosh yeshiva* at home just before it was time to go to *daven Maariv* in the yeshiva. The *rosh yeshiva* said to Rav Arzi, "Come, let me show you how one should treat his wife." He entered the kitchen and told the *rebbetzin*, "I am going to *Maariv* now and will be back right after the *davening*."

When Rav Arzi asked what the *rosh yeshiva* had meant to teach him, Rav Shapira explained, "When you leave your house, it is not enough to tell your wife where you are going. You should also say when you will be back. And you should abide by what you said by coming home on time!"

Tip 1:
Comedy

Tip 2:
Communication, Conversation

Tip 3:
Common Sense

Tip 4:
Compromise, Causation

Tip 5:
Caring, Compassion, Courtesy

Tip 6:
Commonality, Compatibility, Commitment

Tip 7:
Camaraderie, Companionship

Attitude is a little thing
that makes a big difference!

"I am a Yankees fan," a first-grade teacher tells the *cheder* class. "Who likes the Yankees?"

Everyone raises a hand except little Yossi.

"Yossi," the teacher says, surprised. "Why didn't you raise your hand?"

"I'm not a Yankees fan."

"Well, if you're not a Yankees fan, then what team do you like?"

"The Red Sox."

"Why in the world are you a Red Sox fan?"

"Because my *mamma* and *tatte* are Red Sox fans."

"That's no reason to be a Red Sox fan," the teacher replies, annoyed. "You don't have to be just like your parents. What if your mom and dad were morons? What would you be then?"

"A Yankees fan!"

Attitude, Honor, Respect

> They have been married a few short weeks and the wife is
> trying out her first attempt at homemade cinnamon rolls.
> After several minutes at breakfast with no reaction from
> her husband, she finally asks, "Honey, if I baked these rolls
> commercially, how much do you think I could get for one
> of them?"
>
> Without looking up from his newspaper, he replies,
> "About ten years!"

Matrimony was defined by Heinrich Heine as "the high sea for which no compass
has yet been invented!" As usual, Heine, a hopelessly assimilated German Jew
from nineteenth-century Dusseldorf, got it wrong.

Jewish tradition provides the compass for a successful union, and places the
search for *shalom bayis* on the top of the matrimonial to-do list.

Since "no two people think alike,"[1] the Torah, fully aware of the fragility of
human nature, demands that, in order to create lasting goodwill, spouses practice
sincere mutual cooperation.[2]

This approach creates a calming homely pace, an atmosphere at peace with
itself, an attitude that molds *shalom bayis*. This mindset is the sum of your man-
nerisms, your *persona* in words and deeds.

And nothing is more attractive than a positive attitude! As the Lubavitcher
Rebbe would often say, "*Tracht gut, un es vet zein gut* (Think good, and it will be
good)!"

When does attitude start? At the front door!

"Enter not a house suddenly!" urge our Sages, and, once inside, proceed only
with "caution and humility." Oh, and by the way: you should also leave in the
same manner, after being as decorous as possible while inside.[3]

What's the test for good manners?

Solomon ben Yehuda Ibn Gabirol, the eleventh-century philosopher and

---

1.   *Brachos* 58a.
2.   *Yoma* 23a; *Megilla* 28a; *Derech Eretz Zuta* 8.
3.   *Pesachim* 112a; *Ben Sira* 11:8; 2:23; *Pirkei ben Azzai* 2:1.

poet, provides the answer: to patiently tolerate bad ones! An example? Try to understand – instead of trying to be understood!

> The bride was anything but a tidy housekeeper. It didn't bother her much until one evening when her husband called from the hall, somewhat dismayed: "Honey, what happened to the dust on this table? I had a phone number written on it!"

As they say, marriage is like a violin; when the sweet sounds are over, the strings are still attached.

In order to create the right attitude at home, the sounds of these post-*chuppa* strings must be attuned to a more mature courtship. In this light, the *kesuba* certificate is basically a mutual work permit. The chores? Respect and honor.[4]

A house shorn of respect and honor is a house unfit for marital harmony.

Rabbi Dov Heller, a Harvard philosophy graduate and disciple of Aish HaTorah's Rabbi Noah Weinberg, gives some old-fashioned advice of respect: stand up when your spouse enters the room.

The Talmud puts *kavod* (honor, respect) for a spouse ahead of love, which it sees as a "vulnerable and fragile" emotion. The word *kavod* is derived from the same Hebrew root as *kaveid* (heavy, weighty), implying that its objective existential "weight" supports *shalom bayis*.

"Many," reminds the Midrash, "embark on matrimony; most succeed, some come to grief!"[5]

Grief, anguish and heartache fill any vacuum formed by the absence of mu-

---

4. Respect must extend to your extended family, especially your spouse's parents, despite the popularity of in-law jokes. (If you miss your mother-in-law, take another shot! The difference between in-laws and outlaws is that outlaws are wanted! Last week I went on a pleasure trip – I took my mother-in-law to the airport!) It takes enormous patience, maturity and fortitude to handle meddling *mishpacha*, but the challenge must be met and overcome for the sake of *shalom bayis*. What to do when *kibud av v'em* (honoring parents) contradicts *shalom bayis* (marital harmony)? There is no universal answer. You must juggle each principle. However, the Rambam and *Shulchan Aruch* writes that neither spouse can force the other to allow "the parents" to move in – or even visit (*Hilchos Ishus* 13, 14; *Shulchan Aruch, Even Ha'ezer* 74:9–10).

5. *Bamidbar Rabba* 9:4.

tual respect and honor. Their departure opens the gates for the eager enemies of *shalom bayis*: ego and hubris, tyranny and dominance, abuse and disrespect.

"To regard one's own opinion as the best is evil pride," writes the fifteenth-century's *Orchos Tzadikim*, "since such an attitude bars progress!"

> Sammy told his wife that a husband is like fine wine – they both get better with age. So she locked him in the cellar!

Just like a body, a marriage needs constant nourishment. Spousal harmony needs to be fed and clothed, a consistent recipe and wardrobe of patience, restraint, tolerance, self-control – and sharing.

"The one who says, 'What is mine is mine and what is yours is yours' is mediocre…. The one who says, 'What is mine is yours and what is yours is yours' is pious."[6]

Sharing equals unity. Unity equals friendship. Friendship equals peace.

The chassidic rebbe was giving a *shiur* on attitude. "In every life there is a fight between two wolves. One is fear, anger, envy, greed, arrogance, self-pity, resentment, deceit. The other is joy, serenity, humility, confidence, generosity, truth, gentleness, compassion."

One student asks, "Rebbe, which wolf will win?"

The Rebbe replies, "The one you feed!"

> The man was in no shape to drive, so he wisely left his car parked and walked home. As he was walking along unsteadily, he was stopped by a cop. "What are you doing out here at 2:00 a.m.?" asked the officer.
>
> "I'm going to a lecture."
>
> "Oh, yeah? And who is going to give a lecture at this hour?"
>
> "My wife!"

The Rebbe of Chabad at 770 saw a link between family unity and national peace: "Unless there is unity in the family, there can be no unity of the Jewish people…. Needless to say, the said unity must be a constant one, without interruptions. This is to say, it must be expressed not only on certain days of the year, or certain hours of the day, but in *every day* of the year, and in *every hour* of the day."

---

6.   *Pirkei Avos* 5:14.

To be preoccupied with yourself is a guarantee for marital discord.

The Hebrew word for "I" consists of the same letters as the Hebrew word for "nothing." In his poem "The Two Rabbis," the great nineteenth-century American writer John Greenleaf Whittier waxed lyrical: "Heaven's gate is shut to him who comes alone!"

Adds Hillel: "If I am only for myself, what am I?"[7] A selfish spouse! *Sefer Chassidim* (Book of the Pious), a highly valuable religious guide that contains the teachings of three leaders of twelfth- to thirteenth-century German chassidism, is blunt: the prayers of those who ignore the needs of others "are not heard"![8]

Here's the essence: when you get married, it's time to move out of the center and make way for others. Here's another tip: the right choice is when each half can honestly say, "You bring out the best in me!"

As that old Yiddish proverb, adapted from the Midrash,[9] goes: No barber can cut his own hair!

> Wife: Do you want dinner?
> Husband: Sure, what are my choices?
> Wife: *Yes* or *no.*

The what's-yours-is-mine-and-what's-mine-is-mine attitude is a recipe for marital misery and domestic disaster. This attitude serves no useful purpose; in fact, it's guaranteed to exacerbate and irritate.

A state of *shalom bayis* cannot coexist within a state of selfishness.

Koheles was the master of the attitude of discipline ("For everything there is a season").[10] In other words, no one is born with attitude; you must nurture it to maturity; and once matured, a good, healthy attitude turns contagious (those who wish to sing always find a song!) and becomes one of the keys to unlock the secrets of *shalom bayis.*

It was his sheer optimism that inspired Irving Berlin to pen the lyrics, "Got no checkbooks, got no banks, Still I'd like to express my thanks.... I've got the sun in the morning and the moon at night!"

William James, the pioneering American psychologist and master pragma-

---

7.   *Bereishis* 4:7; *Pirkei Avos* 2:4.
8.   *Sefer Chassidim,* No. 1023.
9.   *Vayikra Rabba* 14:9.
10.   *Koheles* 3:1, 8.

tist, was convinced that "the greatest discovery...is that human beings can alter their lives by altering their attitudes of mind." As they say, "As you think, so shall you be!"

Of course, the Torah told us this several thousand years earlier with the formulation of free will.[11]

If you have the will to make your marriage work, you've achieved half your success; if you don't, you've achieved all your failure. In other words: if you *choose* to be a good husband, you will be; if you *choose* to be a good wife, you shall be.

Or as that slang saying puts it: When you feel dog tired at night, it may be because you've growled all day long!

> "My husband and I have a great relationship," Sarah tells her friends after thirty years of marriage. "He was a communications major in college and I majored in theater arts. He communicates real well – and I just act like I'm listening!"

To Sir Winston Churchill, hero of World War II, attitude was "a little thing that makes a big difference!"

In marriage, it makes *all* the difference – especially when you make it upbeat, positive, optimistic, Nachum Ish Gamzu-style: "This too is for the good!"[12]

Honor, according to Mishlei, must be preceded by humility.[13]

Respect and honor lead to gratitude, better communication, more understanding. Treating your spouse respectfully sets the tone of the home, relaxes a spouse's potential anxiety of being unappreciated, and prevents the dysfunctional fear of being misunderstood. When you are unfailingly respectful it shows that you accept the human frailty of imperfections. This attitude reduces vanity and emphasizes the relationship, leaving no room for selfishness to take hold.

With mutual respect and honor a fragile *shalom bayis* no longer becomes the victim of unreasonable and unrealistic demands upon the other.

These core values differentiate the Torah from Western culture's emphasis on being polite, which derives from the Latin *politus* (to polish). Polishing perfects the surface only; Judaic *middos* and manners go far deeper, into the psyche itself.

Remember: in the *yehi ratzon* prayer said after reading the Torah, God is

---

11.   *Pirkei Avos* 3:15; *Midrash Tanchuma, Pikudei* 3.
12.   *Taanis* 21a.
13.   *Mishlei* 15:33.

asked to protect Torah scholars "*and* their wives." According to Rashi, Adam's descent from a state of grace into disgrace resulted from not fully appreciating Eve.[14]

Dozens of major Torah giants (including Rabbi Akiva, Akiva Eiger and Yechezkel Landau) credited their wives for their Torah achievements. Before Rav Isser Zalman Meltzer gave his weekly *shiur* to his students, which he prepared with great intensity, he first repeated it to his wife!

> A sad-looking Freda is confiding in her friend that she isn't happy in her marriage. "What's wrong?" her friend asks.
>
> "Well, from the day of the *chuppa*, Robert has been trying to change me. He got me to stop drinking and smoking. He taught me how to cut down on my compulsive shopping habits. He encouraged me to go to Torah classes, do more mitzvos, *chesed*, and help the kids with their homework. Oh, he also encouraged me to go to gourmet cooking classes and now I'm a great cook. He showed me how to dress well, how to enjoy the fine arts, relax with classical music and he even taught me how to make money on the stock market!"
>
> "Wow!" her friend replies. "So why are you so bitter? Because he spends too much time trying to change you?"
>
> "Oh, no, I'm not bitter," Freda replies, "but now that I'm so improved, I don't think he's good enough for me anymore."

After creating a companion from Adam's rib, God invites Adam to give her a name.

Adam chooses the word *isha*, as close to *ish* (man) as can be, in order to emphasize that both are parts that "bond," as if they were respectfully one.

This inspired the Mishna's ben Zoma to ask, "Who is honored?" and to answer, "He who honors!"[15]

In his sefer *Moreh B'etzba*, Rabbi Chaim Yosef Dovid Azulai (*Chida*), described the efforts of "pursuing peace" as "the spice of life," and listed the priorities:

---

14.   Rashi, *Bereishis* 3:12.
15.   *Pirkei Avos* 4:1.

first within our families, then our extended families, and only then among our friends, neighbors and strangers.

The home gets top priority, he explains, because strife drives away the *Shechina*, and thus couples must be careful to preserve the peace between them.

> One night a wife found her husband standing over their newborn baby's crib. Silently she watched him. As he stood looking down at the sleeping infant, she saw on his face a mixture of emotions: disbelief, doubt, delight, amazement, enchantment, skepticism.
>
> Touched by this unusual display and the deep emotions it aroused, with eyes glistening she slipped her arms around her husband.
>
> "A penny for your thoughts," she whispered in his ear.
>
> "It's amazing!" he replied. "I just can't see how anybody can make a crib like that for only $33.45!"

In Europe, it was a Lubavitch custom that just before a newlywed couple moved into their new home, children from the local Talmud Torah would come and learn *alef beis* there. This was the couple's *chanukas habayis* (dedication of a house), a festive fitting beginning of a new house in Israel, considered a mini-sanctuary for God.[16]

To the Brisker Rav, beginnings were extremely important. They had to be as perfect as possible because they set the tone that lasts for years.

The Vilna Gaon was so meticulous to "start right" that when he built his *shul* he demanded that even the ax handles be manufactured by God-fearing individuals.

When Ner Israel, Baltimore, built their *beis medrash*, the *rosh yeshiva*, Rav Yaakov Ruderman, wanted to "get off on the right foot," so he urged everyone not to speak any *devarim beteilim* (idle chatter) in the *beis medrash* for at least the first week!

---

16.   It is called a *chanukas habayis* after the inaugural seven-day dedication of the *Mishkan* ("And it was on the eighth day..."), the day when Aaron took over from Moshe (*Vayikra* 9:1; *Toras Menachem, Hisvaaduyos,* vol. 5; *Sefer Hasichos 5748,* vol. 2).

> The young couple moved into their first apartment. As the
> wife was unpacking, the husband climbed on a chair in the
> kitchen to hang up an embroidered sign that read, "GOD
> BLESS OUR HAPPY HOME."
>
> The wife yelled out from the other room, "Hey, it goes
> on the other wall, you *schlemiel!*"

The inclusion of God into the marital home is derived from the saga of Eliezer, sent as Avraham's agent to find a wife for his son Yitzchak.

On two occasions, the Torah tells us that Eliezer is accompanied by an angel ("He will send His angel *before you* and you will take a wife for my son from there," and "He will send His angel *with you* and *make your journey successful* and you will take a wife for my son from my family and my father's house").[17]

Why twice?

The angel goes first, up front, to lead the way with Divine guidance. After the match is made, we are reminded that the angel's job is not done.[18] There is still a need for Divine Providence (described as the angel going together with you) to guide the marital relationship, as an active partner, for a peaceful future (so that God will make your way successful!).

For a marriage to have blessings and success, each one of its three partners – husband, wife, God – must be devoted to the other two ("A man cannot live without a woman, a woman cannot live without a man, and the two of them cannot live without the presence of God").[19]

While Sarah was alive, God's presence hovered over their home of *shalom*. It

---

17.   *Bereishis* 24:7, 40.

18.   Does the custom of the betrothal ring date to these times? No. Eliezer's betrothal was done with jewelry, not rings. The first time we hear of the *minhag* of placing a ring on the right forefinger is in the writings of Rabbi Elazar of Worms (1165–1238), and in the sefer *Teshuvos Maharam Mintz*, 109, and *Nachalas Shiva* 12:2. Some Sephardim placed the ring on the left middle finger, akin to winding the *tefillin* strap around this finger, as an expression of the bond between bride, groom and God. Jewish mystics place the ring on the right finger because the "right side" represents giving and loving-kindness. The *Aruch HaShulchan* (27:4) says that all customs are valid (Rokeach 351; Darkei Moshe, *Even Ha'ezer* 27, 3; Rema, *Even Ha'ezer* 27:1; Gra, *Even Ha'ezer*, 5; Be'er Heitev, *Even Ha'ezer* 1; Maharil 64b, Maharam Mintz 109; *Tikunei Zohar* 5, 10, 21).

19.   *Brachos* 9:1.

was an abode of amazing hospitality, a center of *chesed*; the Friday night candle burned from one Shabbas to the next. But when Sarah passed away, all of these attributes left.

The house of Avraham had lost its spark, its driving force, its wisdom. None returned until their son Yitzchak married Rivka, the paragon of kindness and goodness.

The rabbis describe the two golden cherubs that Moshe made by divine command for the Tabernacle, between which the the Divine Presence "dwelled," as being in the image of loving wife and husband.

Over the centuries our sages went out of their way to ensure that their own marriages were the epitome of *shalom*, respect, honor, dedication and dignity, as a shining example of both gentle personal behavior and communal responsibility.[20]

> Sammy to his friend: "My wife says I'm too extravagant and that if anything ever happens to her, I'll have to resort to begging just to feed the kids."
>
> "Wow! So, what did you say?"
>
> "I told her I'd be fine. I mean, since I've been married, look at all the experience I've got!"

Remember: *shalom bayis* is hereditary. What you model for your children is what they will know.

(Did you hear about the invisible man who married the invisible woman? Apparently, the children were not much to look at either!)

After you have read all the books on raising children, listened to all the Torah tapes on chinuch, and attended all the shiurim on good parenting, here's the *tachlis* (bottom line): the best gift you can give your children is a happy home.

Your children see how their parents, the major role models of their lives, treat each other – and will do the same in their own marriages. So the wisest thing you can give your children is a healthy marriage within a safe and encouraging Jewish environment.

"Train up a child in the way he should go and when he is old, he will not depart from it!"[21]

---

20. *Yevamos* 65b; *Bamidbar* 5:11–31; *Sefer Hachinuch*, No. 364, 453.
21. *Mishlei* 22:6.

When Moshe asks the tribes of Reuven and Gad why they want to stay on the far side of the Jordan River, they reply, "for our cattle and for our children."

Moshe gives his permission, but reverses the order, saying they can stay "for your children and for your cattle" – showing that family must always come first, before business or material interests.[22]

Traditionally, the obligation to teach Torah to a child is the father's, but that's not the whole story. From the words of the wisest of the wise, Shlomo Hamelech, we are told, "Never abandon the Torah of your mother!"[23]

Isn't this a contradiction? Not at all. It acknowledges the reality of a Torah home.

The father's teaching process is a technical, analytical, intellectual process. In the absence of wisdom seen and felt, it's insufficient. Especially in the early years, those of *tzarich imo* (when the child needs its mother), only the wife's warmth and wisdom can mold sterling *middos* and shape character, without which the Torah of the father is emotionally empty.

Rav Shimshon Raphael Hirsch explains the contrast: man was formed from cold earth; woman was created from living and warm tissue. Thus she has a "head start" in warmth, compassion and empathy.

And so Shlomo Hamelech elaborates his point: "Her wisdom built her home!"[24] Indeed, in the desert, none of the Jewish women participated in the sins of the golden calf, nor the spies' discouraging report of the Land of Israel.

In other words: a father's role, to build (knowledge), can only begin after the mother has laid the strong foundation (*middos*).[25]

> The father is giving his young boy a *mussar shmuess* on the values of life. "Son, God put us here on earth to help others."
>
> "Oh, I see," the boy replies. After a few minutes of deep thought, he turns to his father and says, "Then what are the others here for?"

---

22. *Bamidbar* 32:16, 24.
23. *Devarim* 6:7; *Mishlei* 1:8.
24. *Mishlei* 9:1.
25. Because a child's natural tendency is towards the mother, the Torah compensates for this normal inclination by placing the father first in its commandment to honor parents.

A good spouse usually makes a good parent. And since children instinctively look to their parents as mentors, parents must make themselves worthy of emulation. How?

By incubating *shalom bayis*, the cornerstone of *chinuch banim u'banos* (educating sons and daughters).[26]

Says the Talmud: "It is incumbent on a man to consume food and drink that cost *less* than he can afford, to wear clothes that he *can* afford, and to show honor to his wife and children *beyond* what he can afford."[27]

In other words, domestic attitude is sensed.

True *shalom* is "felt" in the air, like *mazon kol haneshama*, a life force, with each breath that you take; it's the same mystic spirituality that exists in the unique air in the Land of Israel that makes one wise.

If spousal bliss exists in the home, domestic harmony is felt – *especially* by young children – in the very air they breathe. It becomes an important part of their consciousness as they grow up.

If you mistreat your spouse, not only are you destroying your own tranquility but you are depriving your children (and their children) of the tools they will themselves need to build their own homes of *shalom bayis*.

As S.J. Perelman put it: You don't know how much you don't know until your children grow up and tell you how much you don't know!

> Chani comes home from the first day of school with a note from her teacher that says, "If you promise not to believe everything your child says happens at school, I'll promise not to believe everything she says happens at home!"

---

26. When the head of the US Census Bureau retired, he said he wanted to spend more time with his 2.4 children! The minimum Torah commandment is to have at least one boy and one girl, but this was extended on the basis of Isaiah's "He did not create chaos; He formed it to be inhabited" (*Yevamos* 61b; *Yeshayahu* 45:18). Having a child is an absolute obligation. When King Chizkiyahu the righteous looked into the future and saw he would father a wicked son, he refused to marry. God sent Yeshayahu to warn Chizkiyahu that this sin was unacceptable. Chizkiyahu repented and married the prophet's daughter – and had an evil son (Menashe). However, through Menashe the chain of the House of David endured.

27. *Chullin* 84b.

In order to raise children so that they will grow up to be good spouses, the Steipler Rav told parents to train their children in *anava, tznius, hachna'a, temimus* and *yashrus*, the traits of humility, modesty, self-conquest, simplicity (being "down to earth," non-scheming, uncomplicated) and straightness (being fair and honest with others).

When asked what one should look for in a *shidduch*, Rav Yaakov Kamenetsky replied, "A spouse should have two qualities, *gezunt un gut*, 'health and goodness,' for these are the two things we give over to our children."

And in order that good *middos* be passed down through the generations, the Torah advises one to "marry early, that we may teach our children's children."[28]

When asked to explain the phrase "your tent is in peace," the rabbis of the Talmud say it refers to "him who loves his wife as himself and honors her more than himself, who leads his children in the right path, and arranges for their early marriage."[29]

Imitation is education. Oscar Wilde, the famous Irish author and maven of wit, got it right. He said that "example is not the main thing in influencing others – it is the *only* thing!"

> On the first day of school, the rebbe said to his *talmidim*, "There are three words that I don't allow in my class. One is *gross*, one is *awesome*, and the other is *cool*."
>
> A few moments go by and a *talmid* asks, "So, Rebbe, what are the words?"

In fact, never worry that children aren't *listening* to you; worry that they are *watching* you!

And what should they see? Respect, honor, consideration; in short, mutual *kavod*, an obligation stated clearly in your *kesuba*, a legal contract.

When the Rambam codified this attitude into law (in his *Hilchos Ishus*, Laws of Marriage), the obligation to honor was first placed on the husband to his wife (as the Talmud says, "honor her *more* than yourself!"),[30] and, the logic goes, she will then surely reciprocate.

---

28.   Yishmael ben Elisha, on *Devarim* 4:9, *Kiddushin* 61a.
29.   *Yevamos* 62b.
30.   Ibid.

Shalom bayis requires immediate integration from the time of the *vort* (engagement).

Success does not spring from *finding* the right mate, but from *being* the right mate.

Descartes's famous existential philosophical formula (*Cogito ergo sum*, "I think therefore I am") is foreign to a Torah that sees community as key. Judaism not only demands that all Jews interact, but stretches that concept to its mystical-spiritual goal: *Kol Yisroel areivim zeh lazeh*, "All Jews are guarantors, one for another!"[31]

Rav Yaakov Mecklenberg of Koenigsberg, Germany, author of *Hakesav V'hakabala*, traced the Hebrew root of *toda* (thanks) to *yad* (hand), a reflection of the custom of shaking hands to "seal the deal."

The odds of achieving *shalom bayis* if one enters a marriage solely for *personal* gain are between zero and nil. Unless "we" replaces "I," the marital horizon is scattered with land mines. One is none: life's triumphs are "*our*" simchas, tragedies "*ours*" to absorb together.

Remember: "I" is always a *singular* (selfish) pronoun; it can never become a functioning part of the collectivity of a spouse and family (appropriately, the major Jewish organization is called OU, not O-Me).

The Torah is very clear about the threat to communal and individual harmony posed by the attitude of *Looking Out for Number One*. It reduces the problem to one single word at the beginning of the Torah portion of the rebellious Korach: "And Korach took..."[32]

We're not even told what he took. Once a taker, always a taker, never a giver![33]

---

31. *Shevuos* 39a.
32. *Bamidbar* 16:1–18:32.
33. The *Shulchan Aruch*, in an astute observation that in reaching out to others we find ourselves, does not exempt a Jewish beggar-pauper from giving charity to others, no matter how small the amount. Rabbi Shlomo Efraim of Prague, the seventeenth-century Torah commentator known as the *Kli Yakar*, points out the Torah's choice of words: instead of "giving" sacrifices, the repeated reference is to "taking offerings" to the Sanctuary. Why? Every element of giving incorporates an aspect of taking. Giving to others with a smile and a pleasant disposition creates the atmosphere of *nachas ruach* (contentment of spirit), a reward within itself (*Yoreh Deah* 248:1).

The Hebrew root of *ahava* (love), Rav Shimshon Raphael Hirsch notes, is the same as "to offer" or "to bring forth," suggesting that to love is to give.[34]

A fourteenth-century *mussar* moralist advised, "Both in writing and in speaking, say 'he and I,' not 'I and he.'" Arthur Guiterman, twentieth-century American poet, famously reduced all of good manners to eight words: Forget Yourself and Think of Those Around You!

Remember: when Avraham reached Canaan, the first thing he did was set up his wife's tent (*vayeit ohala*),[35] before attending to his own needs.

The continuity of *shalom bayis* requires the transformation of each individual spouse to the level of no longer instinctively reacting as an individual, but rather making the crucial change from "me" to "we."

> Josh found his *bashert* later in life and by the time he married Susie, he was pretty confirmed in his habits and routines.
>
> When it came time to buy the tickets for the cruise Josh and Susie planned to take for their honeymoon, he absent-mindedly bought just one ticket, as he was accustomed to do.
>
> Susie was distraught when she saw the lone ticket and Josh had to think fast. "Oh, my goodness," he blurted out, "I forgot to buy a ticket for myself!"

The relationship is either an "organic" whole, where the sum is more stable than the parts, or the marital misery of a dysfunctional household of two individuals living their own lives under the same roof.

Koheles reminds us, "Two is better than one!"[36] – but the street Yiddishists in Europe expressed it much better: One grape does not make a bunch!

Some married folks enter a room and say, "Here *I* am!" Others enter and say, "Ah, there *you* are!"

One husband sees his wife fall down and berates her, "Why are you always

---

34. In the contemporary world, with a divorce rate over 50 percent, cynicism rules. The *New York Times* once ran a crossword puzzle with a marriage theme titled, "Love – American Style?" wherein the answers "dating game" and "love connection" led straight to "divorce court"!
35. *Bereishis* 12:8. See "The Midrash on O's and H's" later in this chapter.
36. *Koheles* 4:9.

falling? Can't you walk properly?!" Other more sensitive, more concerned husbands beat the ground saying, "What did you do to my wife?!"

> Moishie's friends bought him a parrot as a gift, but the parrot had a very bad attitude and a foul vocabulary. Moishie tried to change the bird's attitude by speaking politely and playing soft music. But nothing worked. One day Moishie lost his patience and screamed at the parrot, but that only made matters worse. The bird only became ruder. Finally, in a moment of desperation, Moishie grabbed the parrot and threw him in the freezer to get a minute of peace. For several minutes the bird was heard swearing, squawking, kicking and screaming. Then, suddenly, there was absolute silence. Moishie was frightened that he might have hurt the bird and quickly opened the freezer door.
>
> The parrot carefully stepped out onto Moishie's extended arm. Perfectly calm, the bird said, "I am terribly sorry that I offended you with my language and my actions and I beg your forgiveness. I will do my best to change my attitude and correct my behavior, and promise that it will never happen again. Oh, by the way, may I ask what the chicken did?"

One last thing about attitude: never take the other for granted.

The *Chazon Ish* nudged husbands to show constant sensitivity and authentic admiration for what their wives do for them, their house, their children. A lack of appreciation is the catalyst for isolating yourself in marriage.[37]

With an eye on *shalom bayis*, *Mishlei* warns, "*L'taava yevakesh nifrad* (self-indulgence will pursue separateness)."[38]

Every human being has faults and insecurities – nobody's perfect. *Shalom bayis* requires a sense of attachment, and a feeling that spouses are *ishto k'gufo*, considered as one person (literally, "his wife is like his [own] body").

This is not just a Torah imperative, but a pragmatic one as well.

---

37. *Chullin* 84b; *Hilchos Deios* 5:10; *Yevamos* 62b; *Sanhedrin* 76b; *Bava Metzia* 59a; Rambam, *Hilchos Ishus* 5:19; *Sota* 11; *Kesubos* 72a; *Vayikra* 25:17; *Sefer Hachinuch*, No. 341; *Kiddushin* 31a; R. Shlomo Wolbe, *Maamarei Hadracha L'Chasanim.*
38. *Mishlei* 18:1.

Good spouses provide "backup." Encouragement is a trait of *hakaras hatov,* "recognizing good," another Torah imperative. Why? Because it's a basic human need to feel appreciated.

Rav Asher Zeev Werner of Tiberias would serve his wife a cup of coffee and bring her breakfast before doing anything for himself or his guests. Rabbi Shlomo Heiman, *rosh yeshiva* of Torah Vodaas, had a *rebbetzin* who went out every evening to raise funds for poor orphans. So every night, of his own volition, the busy *rosh yeshiva* turned down the beds, boiled tea and prepared cake for her return.

Respect one another, urges Eleazar ben Azaria.[39] Why?

Because *shalom bayis* is identified by how partners treat each other. Selfishness and harmony in the home cannot coexist. Self-centeredness is simply frozen compassion.

> After the wedding, the successful father-in-law is walking his new son-in-law through his factory. "To show you how much we care for you as part of our family," he says, "I'm making you a fifty-fifty partner in my business. All you have to do is come in every day and learn the operations."
>
> "You know," the new son-in-law replies, "I really hate factories. I can't stand the noise."
>
> "OK, well, then you can work in the offices where it's quiet and tidy."
>
> "Well, to tell you the truth, I hate office work. I have no patience to be stuck behind a desk all day."
>
> "I don't get it," says the flabbergasted father-in-law. "I just made you half-owner of a profitable business, but you won't work in the factory or the office. What am I going to do with you?"
>
> "It's easy. Buy me out!"

In creating the right atmosphere at home, remember: when you are thoughtful, sincere, and respectful, you are more likely to be respected.[40]

As they say: What goes around, comes around!

---

39. *Pirkei ben Azzai* 1:4.
40. *Kiddushin* 31a; *Megilla* 12b; Rambam, *Hilchos Ishus* 15:20; Rema, *Even Ha'ezer* 69:7.

Respect elicits counter-respect; honor escalates honor, in line with the rabbinic adage of *midda k'neged midda*, "measure for measure"; others treat you the way you treat them.[41]

In short: choose your love, then love your choice!

Don't be distracted; if you think the grass is greener on the other side, it's probably because they look after it better!

> A farmer in a small Polish shtetl decides to buy the property around his farm and goes to his neighbors offering them animals as payment – a horse where the man is the boss, a chicken where the woman is the boss. After several purchases, he walks up to an ol' Jewish couple sitting in their garden and asks, "Who's the boss around here?"
>
> "I am," the man says.
>
> "I have a black horse and a brown horse for your property; which one would you like?"
>
> The man thinks for a minute and says, "The black one."
>
> "No, no, no!" the wife yells, "get the brown one!"
>
> "Here's your chicken," says the farmer.

---

41. *Sota* 9b.

The *Netziv* on Torah Study and *Shalom Bayis*

The author of *Torah Temima*, in his historical work *Mekor Baruch*, relates a story that involved his uncle, Rabbi Naftoli Tzvi Yehuda Berlin (the *Netziv*, an acronym meaning "pillar," by which the famed *rosh yeshiva* of Volozhin was known). A distinguished and charitable businessman, who had at one time been recognized as a *lamdan*, came to the *Netziv* to discuss a personal problem. While he was universally respected as a prominent citizen of his community and made an excellent livelihood, no sooner would he cross the threshold of his house than he became a nonentity. His wife completely dominated the household and ignored him, except to berate him. He felt like a stranger in his own home, which was a source of endless anguish to him.

The *Netziv* asked him if he set aside specific times during the day for Torah study. The man replied that he had become so involved in his business that he did not have the time to establish a *seder*. The *Netziv* stated emphatically, "You must resolve to establish a regular *seder* for a few hours every day – no matter how busy you might be. You must immerse yourself in your Talmudic studies and make it an integral, inviolable part of your life. If you heed my advice, I can assure you that your situation will improve greatly."

The *Mekor Baruch* relates that when he subsequently met his cousin, Rabbi Chaim Berlin, the son of the *Netziv*, he asked him about how this incident was resolved. Reb Chaim replied, "I am familiar with the entire story, and I know the merchant personally. As a matter of fact, whenever his business brings him to Moscow, he stops by to tell me how grateful he is to my father for his wonderful advice. His entire home life has changed ever since he began setting aside time for intensive Torah study. His wife now respects him and treats him with the utmost deference."

The advice of the *Netziv* was not some magical formula, but rather a logical suggestion. Once the woman saw that her husband had reordered his priorities and that Torah had assumed a place of prominence in his life, she realized that she was married to a truly respectable individual and accorded him the honor such a person is entitled to.

The *Chazon Ish* on Hanging the Laundry

There was a young newlywed yeshiva man who was walking around looking rather depressed. Seeing this, Rabbi Refoel Dovid Auerbach sat down with the man to encourage him and find out what was troubling him. The man finally blurted out his problem: "I was hoping that my marriage would help me grow in Torah, but since my wedding, my wife gives me chore after chore. First, she asks me to take out the garbage and then to do some shopping. Today she asked me to hang the laundry! It has gotten to the point where I can no longer concentrate on my learning!"

Since the young newlywed appeared sincere, he said to him, "Let us take your problem to the *Chazon Ish*. He will surely be able to advise you."

Together they went to the *Chazon Ish*'s home, and there the man once again burst into tears, recounting all the chores he had at home and his inability to concentrate on his learning. However, to Rabbi Refoel Dovid's surprise, the *Chazon Ish*, with his hands on his chin, just sat there and smiled.

When the man finished speaking, the *Chazon Ish* replied: "There are only two in the world who know for certain whether your intentions are sincere. The first is, obviously, *HaKadosh Boruch Hu*, and the second is your dear wife. I am certain that if your wife would see that you truly wanted to spend every spare minute delving deeper into the Torah, not only would she stop requesting your help but she would go all out to help you and prevent any disturbance. Therefore, I must conclude that, at this point, she does not see this in you. She probably observes that you waste time here and there with trivial things, so she says to herself, 'If he has time on his hands, he might as well help me.' My guarantee to you is that if you resolve to truly engross yourself in the sea of Torah, your wife will not only want to assist you, she will do whatever is in her power to allow you more time to learn."

The man thought about the *Chazon Ish*'s words and resolved to take the dive into the world of pure Torah. Indeed, as the *Chazon Ish* had foreseen, the man's wife went out of her way to take care of his personal matters for him so he could learn undisturbed.

Rav Avrohom Pam
on Taking Peace for Granted

Shalom bayis is not to be taken for granted and left to run its own course. Like a beautiful garden it needs constant care and concern. It is interesting that in the *kesuba*, the husband pledges: "I will work, honor, feed, and support you." It would seem that the promise to honor is out of order, for it should have been placed first: "honor, work, feed, and support you."

The fact that "work" is first would seem to indicate that just as supporting one's wife calls for a great investment of time and effort, so too must one work at properly honoring her. It is an aspect of life that does not take care of itself, but can suffer seriously if neglected.

– Rav Avrohom Pam, zt"l, rosh yeshiva Mesivta Torah Vodaas

Rav Moshe Cordovero on Marital *Kavod*

The Arizal said to Rabbi Moshe Cordovero that he had *ruach hakodesh* [Divine knowledge] that if the two of them went from their hometown of Tzfas, Israel, to Jerusalem right away, they would bring Moshiach. Rabbi Cordovero said that he would just tell his wife that he was leaving for Jerusalem.

When he came back, ready to leave, the Arizal said that, in the time he had taken to say good-bye to his wife, the opportunity had passed and it was too late. Rabbi Yisroel Salanter, known as the father of the *mussar* movement, said that we see from this that you cannot bring Moshiach if it means doing so on the *cheshbon* of one's wife. It was more important that Rabbi Cordovero give respect to his wife than bring Moshiach with the great Arizal!

Unity and Faith and Patience!

In a small town there was a severe drought. The community shuls each *davened* separately for rain, but to no avail. The tears and prayers failed to unlock the sealed gates of Heaven, and for months, no rains came.

Finally, the town's eldest *rav* held a meeting with prominent community *rabbonim* and lay leaders. "There are two items lacking in our approach: faith and unity. Each one of you must impress upon his congregation the need to believe. If we are united and sincere, our prayers will be answered!"

He declared that all the shuls in the city would join together for a day of *tefilla*. Everyone – men, women and children – would join together for this event. "I assure you," he exclaimed, "that if we meet both criteria – faith and unity – no one will leave that prayer service without getting drenched!"

There was no shul large enough to contain the entire community, so the date was set to gather and daven in a field. For the next few weeks, all the *rabbonim* spoke about *bitachon* (faith) and *achdus* (unity). On the designated day, the entire town gathered in a large field whose crops had long withered from the severe drought. Men, women and children all gathered and anxiously awaited the old *rav* to begin the *atzeres tefilla*.

The elderly *rav* walked up to the podium. His eyes scanned the tremendous crowd that filled the large field and then they dimmed in dismay. The *rav* began shaking his head in dissatisfaction. "This will never work," he moaned dejectedly. "The rain will not come." Slowly he left the podium.

The other *rabbonim* on the dais were shocked. "But Rebbe, everyone is here and they are all united! Surely they must believe that the rains will fall! Otherwise, no one would have bothered to come on a working day!"

The *rav* shook his head slowly and sadly. "No. They don't really believe," he stated. "I scanned the entire crowd. Nobody even brought a raincoat!"

The Midrash on O's and H's

We learn from an explication in *Bereishis Rabba* that a husband should put his wife's needs before his own. When Avraham travels to Canaan, the Torah records that he "pitched his tent."[42]

Hebrew is a compact language that conveys a lot of information in each word. In this verse, "pitched his tent" is rendered in the single word *ohalOH* (his tent). This should be spelled *aleph, heh, lamed* (*ohel*, "tent"), with the vowelization *cholam* ("o") at the end to indicate the masculine possessive (his).

Yet, interestingly, the Torah spells the word *aleph, heh, lamed, heh*. The *heh* at the end is normally used with the vowelization *kamatz* ("ah"), which would indicate the object is "hers," and should therefore mean "her tent."

Hebrew vowels are not indicated with letters, but with *nekudos*, separate diacritical marks; since these are not recorded in the written Torah we rely on the *mesora* (tradition) to know how to pronounce the words. In this case, the *keri*, the oral tradition for how we pronounce this word, is with the vowelization "o," with the simple meaning "his tent."

Yet in the *kesiv*, the written text, the Torah spells the word with an extra *heh* at the end, as if it should be pronounced *ohalAH*, meaning "her tent." The Midrash explains that this letter *heh* in the *kesiv* serves to give us a hint as to the proper way for a husband to honor his wife, by taking care of her needs before his own.

---

42. *Bereishis* 12:8.

The *Chofetz Chaim* on Patience

The *Chofetz Chaim* had a habit of picking out *talmidim* whom he believed needed improvement in various areas of their *avodas Hashem*, and would take them by the hand outside for a stroll around the yeshiva. He would walk with them, warmly discussing the issues that concerned him and offering suggestions how one could improve in these areas.

One boy displayed an exceptional degree of impatience and was short-tempered. He recalls how, "One day, the *Chofetz Chaim* called for me to join him for one of his walks. For the duration of one hour, he repeated one word over and over again: "patience, patience," until the concept became ingrained in my bones. From then on I began to work on perfecting myself, a little bit at a time, until my entire personality changed."

A Lesson from
Reb Yaakov Kamenetsky

Reb Yaakov once went to a fund-raising dinner together with Rabbi Shneur Kotler, *rosh yeshiva* of Lakewood. They were about to enter the front door when Rav Shneur said, "If we go in the front door everyone will stand up for us – let's go in the back way instead."

Rav Shneur was shocked when Reb Yaakov, known for being a great *anav* (very humble), disagreed with him and insisted on going in the front way.

When Rav Shneur asked why, Reb Yaakov explained that when the crowd stood up for them, their own wives, who were sitting inside, would feel honored!

How to Get a *Get,* Amicably

Once, in a bygone era, a Jew came to his *rav* to divorce his wife. As the *rav* had not heard of any marital problems, he was surprised, to say the least. He pressed his visitor, "Can we perhaps arrange a reconciliation? What are your complaints against your wife?"

"No," the Jew told the *rav,* "all has been discussed and now it's time to arrange the *get.*" As to his complaints, he said, "Since the *get* is not yet final, she is still my wife. With all due respect, I will not speak evil of my wife."

The *rav* persisted, "You must have complaints; what claims do you have against your wife?"

"As long as she is still my wife," the man resolutely responded, "I will not speak against her."

Seeing no alternative, the *rav* sadly administered the *get.*

After the divorce proceedings were finished, the *rav* approached the Jew with a final question: "Now that the *get* is completed, will you tell me what your complaints were against your former wife? Why did you want the divorce?"

The man answered the *rav,* "Since the divorce is final, the woman who was my wife is no longer related to me. She is like any other Jew. Why should I speak evil about another Jew?"

Fire and the *Shechina*

Since the world was created using the Hebrew language,[43] the essence of all things is contained within their names. The Gemora explains how the names of man and woman reveal something critical about marriage.[44]

Man is *ish*, spelled *aleph, yud, shin*. Woman is *isha*, spelled *aleph, shin, heh*. Man has one letter of God's name (*yud*) and woman another (*heh*). When a man and woman join together in a wholesome manner, the Shechina (the Divine Presence) rests between them. But when the couple lives without God in their marriage, the *yud* and *heh* are removed, leaving in each name only *aleph* and *shin*: *eish* (fire).

Fire that coexists with the Godly Presence is passion and life, but a fiery relationship without God is a blaze that destroys all in its path.

---

43. *Midrash Tanchuma* 58:28b; *Bereishis Rabba* 31:8.
44. *Sota* 17a.

Tip 1:
Comedy

Tip 2:
Communication, Conversation

Tip 3:
Common Sense

Tip 4:
Compromise, Causation

Tip 5:
Caring, Compassion, Courtesy

Tip 6:
Commonality, Compatibility,
Commitment

Tip 7:
Camaraderie,
Companionship

We make a living by what we get,
but we make a life by what we give!

– Winston Churchill

Esther and Benny, a young newlywed couple, are strolling along Fifth Avenue in Manhattan late at night window shopping. Esther stops in front of an expensive handbag store. "Gee, Benny," she sighs, "I wish I could have one of those handbags."

So Benny takes a brick, smashes the window and hands her a bag. They keep walking until Esther suddenly stops at a high-priced jewelry store. "Gee, Benny, I wish I could have a set of those pearl earrings."

So Benny takes a brick, smashes the window and hands her a set of pearl earrings. They keep walking until Esther spots a high-class furrier store. "Gee, Benny, I wish I could have one of those white mink coats."

"Hey," replies Benny, "what do you think I am…made out of bricks or something?!"

Friendship

> Mendy walks over to the perfume counter and asks for a
> bottle of Chanel No. 5, saying, "It's my wife's birthday."
>   "A little surprise, eh?" the salesgirl smiles.
>   "You bet! She's expecting a cruise!"

"Life has taught us that love does not consist in gazing at each other," writes An-
toine de Saint Exupéry in *Wind, Sand and Stars*, "but in looking outward together
in the same direction!"

The Torah describes the "Going-my-way?" relationship between Avraham
and Sarah as being a couple sharing a common dream: "He brought the men [in
Charan] closer [to God], she brought the women."

A successful marriage is thus not a destination, but a journey. The required
luggage is *shalom bayis* – being united in purpose and spirit, goals and values,
both moving in the same general direction. You don't need to have the same
interests but you need to respect your spouse's differences. Otherwise you're on
a collision course.

If you ask a newly engaged couple why they chose whom they chose, put
your antenna up: there are many "right" answers, but especially impressive and
revealing is the simple truth, "We enjoy each other's company."

Rav Shmuel Berenbaum, the *rosh yeshiva* of Mir, had a long (sixty years), successful marriage. His friends credited the couple's "commonality of purpose."

Married couples enrich their relationship by sharing meaningful experiences and a common philosophy of life and life's purpose, *together*. An example?
Keeping Shabbas, *together*; raising children, *together*; going to *simchas*, *together*,
and so on.

Shalom bayis finds a more natural welcoming home in one built by couples
who purposefully share truly meaningful experiences, allowing them to bond
on a deeper level.

A pot of long-term commonality, stirred with the discipline of family purity
(*taharas hamishpacha*) and sprinkled with shared values and mutual aspirations,
produces a tasty dish of *shalom bayis*.

But the recipe will still come up short without the essential ingredient: friendship!

> A rabbi was called to a Miami Beach nursing home to perform a wedding.
>
> An anxious old man met him at the door. The rabbi sat down to counsel the old man and asked several questions. "Do you love her?"
>
> The old man replied, "I guess."
>
> "Is she a good Jewish woman?"
>
> "I don't know for sure," the old man answered.
>
> "Does she have lots of money?" asked the rabbi.
>
> "I doubt it."
>
> "Then why are you marrying her?" the rabbi asked.
>
> "She can drive at night," the old man said.

If Torah is the common denominator of marriage paths,[1] then friendship and satisfaction (*nachas ruach*) represent the paving stones.

Says *Pirkei Avos*: one of the forty-eight virtues through which Torah is acquired is friendship,[2] with *dibbuk chaverim* literally meaning "cleaving to friends."

In his ethical will, Asher ben Yechiel, thirteenth-century German-Spanish scholar, urged his children, "Never be weary of making friends…. If you have a faithful friend, hold fast to him. Let him not go, for he is a precious possession."

The glue of marital relationships is to be a *chaver*, derived from the Hebrew root *ches-veis-reish*, which means "to be joined" or "to unite."

This is why the blessing sung at the wedding to the bride and groom (*Sameiach tesamach re'im ha'ahuvim*, "Be happy and rejoice, friends and lovers!") includes the term *re'im* (friends). Our Sages understood that in the context of a lasting *shalom bayis* there's nothing superfluous about friendship.

---

1.   The *Chofetz Chaim* wrote an entire book (*Toras Habayis*) on the merits of learning Torah at home (that is why it's important that each home have a considerable library to act as a magnet for further learning at home, and the walls of the home should be lined with "*yiddisher zachin* [Jewish things]," to incubate a constant sense of awareness and respect for a peaceful, homely Jewishness).

2.   *Pirkei Avos* 6:6.

Leah, expecting her first child, was going into the hospital to have surgery and her husband wasn't taking any chances. Prior to her operation, he taped notes all over his wife's body for the surgeon: "Take your time," "Don't cut yourself," "No need to rush," "Wash your hands," etc.

After surgery, when she came back to her hospital bed, he noticed a note taped to her from the doctor: "Hey! Has anyone seen my watch?"

Rav Yosef Chaim Sonnenfeld was so determined not to let his learning and community duties as *rav* of Yerushalayim interfere with paying attention to his wife that he had a daily *shiur* with her (in *Ein Yaakov*).

The *rebbetzin*'s friends asked if they could join but Rav Sonnenfeld was adamant: the time was for his wife only!

In a survey published in the sociological study *The Jewish Wife*,[3] the majority of Jewish women replied to the question "What are you looking for in a prospective mate?" with, "Someone I can talk to."

Despite the fact that the first mitzva is to "be fruitful and multiply,"[4] God clearly outlines the central reason for marriage: "*Lo tov heyot ha'adam l'vado, e'eseh lo eizer k'negdo* (It's not good for man to be alone; I will make him a helpmate)."[5]

The Rambam, Rav Moshe Isserles and Rabbeinu Yaakov ben Asher all agree: the purpose of marriage is not just for procreation but a recognition that human beings require companions in order to mitigate existential and social isolation.

God Himself saw that to combat the helplessness of loneliness, it was necessary to provide companionship for the man He had created (Samuel, an *amoraic* authority, urges marriage as "an obligation" for two more reasons: it "completes" a man, and it's socially necessary in order to establish a household and enter Jewish society as a responsible adult).

---

3. Gwen Gibson Schwartz and Barbara Wyden, *The Jewish Wife* (New York: Peter H. Wyden, Inc., 1969).
4. *Bereishis* 1:28.
5. Ibid. 2:18.

The German-born Rabbi Israel Isserlein ben Petachya, author of the halachic responsa *Terumas Hadeshen*, ruled that it is better to enter into a marriage of bliss with a woman who cannot bear children rather than enter into a marriage of strife with a woman capable of bearing children.[6]

The blessing of friendship, which Moshe ibn Ezra calls "man's greatest gift," is thus the ultimate foundation for *shalom bayis*. Why? Because friends see – and accept – each other's "*shticklach*" (faults, hang-ups, quirks, habits).

> "You'll be sorry," Andy screams at his wife, "I'm going to leave you!"
>
> "Well," she says, "make up your mind; which one is it going to be?"

The sublimity and idealism of *shalom bayis* requires both a physical clinging and a spiritual clinging.

The first time the word *cling* appears in the Torah is in the context of companionship ("He clings to his wife").

By using the same term later in reference to "clinging to" God, the text reminds us that there are three partners (husband, wife, God) in marriage.[7] And only a successful triangulation of all three, who, according to Jewish tradition, even stand side-by-side-by-side under the *chuppa*, produces a lasting and satisfying *shalom bayis*.

"Behold," says the husband to his new wife, "you are made holy to me!"[8]

It is only *after* the couple agree to the ground rules from Sinai that God steps in to help out.

One of God's names, points out the Sfas Emes, is *Eloka*, which has the same Hebrew letters (*alef, lamed, heh*) as *ohel*, "home."

Thus, unless a Jewish home operates God's way, "one toils in vain to build it!"[9]

---

6.   *Terumas Hadeshen* 1:263.
7.   *Devarim* 10:20; *Sota* 17a; *Kiddushin* 30b.
8.   *Yirmiyahu* 2:3.
9.   *Tehillim* 127:1.

It is God's Presence at the *chuppa* (deservedly so because He chose the *bashert!*) that makes marriage worthy of being called *kiddushin*, "conferring of holiness," in the expectation of all involved that the "conferring" will continue throughout the union.

This "guaranteed" match is called *bashert*, which means "fate, destiny" (it is now used for anything fortuitous, such as finding a good job, the perfect house, etc.).

We derive this mysterious notion from the Talmud where Rav teaches that forty days before a male child is born a *bas kol*, "a heavenly voice," declares *bas ploni l'ploni*, "the daughter of so-and-so is meant for this child."[10]

"*Bashert* is *bashert!*" as the Yiddishists would say (in Spanish, it's "*Que sera, sera*").

This belief raises many questions (what about the case of divorce, for example), and even such basic ones as, who hears the announcement, anyway? Jewish tradition says that the future *shadchan*, or friends and relatives, eventually, at the appropriate time, hear the *bas kol* and urge the couple to get married. The other obvious question is this: what's the hurry? Why forty days before birth? Why not later in life, at the bar/bas mitzva?

One answer is that, until the child is born, it's still in the womb and in the hands of God. After birth, the child is raised by the parents. The pre-birth declaration is a reminder that marriages are made in Heaven.

Although it's used more often, *bashert* is not the correct word. Someone else can make a mistake and marry *your bashert*. The more correct term is *zivug*, which connotes one permanent "life partner." You can marry several times – but have only one *zivug!*[11]

---

10.   *Sota* 2a.
11.   The ancient Greeks used their version of *gematria* (*alpha* is one, *beta* is two, etc.) to decide who was *bashert* for whom. For example: if the girl's name added up to 6, and 6 was divisible by 1, 2, and 3, which also added up to 6, they were a predestined couple. If the girl's name added up to 18, and 18 was divisible by 1, 2, 3, 6 and 9, which adds up to 21 (and not 18), they were not meant for each other.

The little six-year-old has never been to a *chuppa* before. Confused, she tugs at her mother's dress. "Yes, what is it?" the mother asks.

"How come, mommy, the bride is all dressed in white?"[12]

"Because this is the happiest day of her life," the mother replies.

After staring at the couple for several more minutes the little girl asks, "Then how come the *chasan* is dressed in black?"

Yosef Zabara, the thirteenth-century scholar and physician from Barcelona, called friendship "one heart in two bodies."

The Russian Binyamin Mandelstamm, in his nineteenth-century sefer *Mishlei Binyamin*, compares friendship to a treasury: "You cannot take from it more than you put into it!"[13]

After our Sages referred to a wife as a *chaveret*, "companion,"[14] the Rambam broke down the term into three levels of friendship: *chaver l'davar*, a down-to-earth reciprocal sharing of duties; *chaver l'daaga*, a relationship of companionship based on sharing experiences, both positive and negative; and *chaver l'deiah*, a true partnership based on the joint pursuit of common goals in life.

---

12. Wearing a white dress, symbol of purity, is only a recent custom. Until the nineteenth century, brides simply wore their best dress, of any color. Blue, associated with fidelity, was popular, and led to the idea of wearing "something old, something new, something borrowed and something blue." "Old" symbolizes the past; "new" looks to the future; "borrowed" is a link with the present.

13. Are there *segulos* for having *shalom bayis*? Some people say parts of *Tehillim* 119 because it begins with letters that spell out *shalom bayis*. Others (e.g., *Likutei Eitzos Aruch Shalom*) claim that *tzedaka* is a *segula*; the Segulas Yisroel advises couples who are fighting to check their *kesubos* for errors, the Mesores Yisroel recommends learning Maseches Succa as a *segula* for peace in the home, and the Bnei Yisaschar says making a *seuda* and dating on Tu b'Av is a traditional *segula*. The final word goes to Rav Avrohom Yaakov Pam from Yeshiva Torah Vodaas: after mentioning the *segula* of the husband setting up the *neiros erev Shabbas* and folding his *tallis* carefully after Shabbas, he suggested that a more effective *segula* for *shalom bayis* is helping with the kids *erev Shabbas* and washing the *cholent* pot.

14. *Malachi* 2:14.

The Rambam also breaks "love" into three categories – those who love for advantage (e.g., a king, business partners, etc.), those who love for comfort (e.g., for security), and those who love for virtue (e.g., in the context of trying to do something good) – and defines the third as the highest form of genuine love.

> Freddie convinces his reluctant wife to go skiing. On the first day he falls and breaks a leg. "Why couldn't this have happened on my last day of skiing?" he complains.
> "This is your last day of skiing!" she replies.

Jewish mystics ask, why does Hebrew use the term *raaya* for "friend," and not *chaver, oheiv*, etc.?

Raaya is a combination of *ra*, the Hebrew word for "evil," and *yud*, the first initial of God's name (*yud-kay-vav-kay*). The attachment of the *yud* counteracts the iniquity and wickedness, producing a high-quality friendship (with such Godly attributes as patience, humility, kindness, forgivingness, etc.) that can withstand any evil that befalls it.

To turn your spouse, in addition to all the other requirements of a spouse, into a lifelong *chaver* is considered the safest investment in *shalom bayis*, a blessing of *chibbur* – a sustained "joint partnership" in the words of German Rabbi Moshe Sofer (*Chasam Sofer*), as reflected in one of the *sheva brachos* given at the *chuppa* that you become *re'im ahuvim*, "beloved friends."

In fact, two out of the seven *sheva brachos* refer to "companionship"; none to having children.

And guess where the last blessing, the only one cast in the form of a petition ("Soon may there be heard..."),[15] which lists no fewer than ten synonyms for happiness (joy, gladness, mirth, exultation, pleasure, delight, love, brotherhood, peace) puts "friendship"?

At the top of the list!

> Beryl complains to his doctor that he isn't able to do all the things around the house that he used to do. When the examination is complete, he says, "*Nu*, Doc, I can take it. Tell me in plain English what is wrong with me."
> "Well, in plain English," the doctor replies, "You're lazy."
> "OK, OK," says Beryl, "now give me the medical term so I can tell my wife."

---

15. The seventh blessing is also the only one that can be said during the *sheva brachos* without a *minyan*, but with at least three men.

A woman once went up to Winston Churchill at a party and said, "If you were my husband I would poison your drink!"

He replied, "If you were my wife I would drink it!"

It was the same Churchill, master of the quick biting wit, who observed, "We make a living by what we get, but we make a life by what we give!" ("If you want to cleave to your friend with love," advises a *mussar* manual, "constantly seek what is good *for him!*").[16]

Giving is not limited only to property.

Giving includes time, energy, concern, knowledge, encouragement, advice, listening, empathy – and friendship!

The Torah does not consider giving to be a passive, reactive activity. Don't wait, sings Shlomo Hamelech, but enthusiastically "*chase* charity and kindness!"[17]

Shalom bayis rewards those who marry to *give* happiness, as well as *receive* it. And it disappoints those who marry based upon selfishness, or just for wealth, prestige, social reasons, vanity, pride or in order to spite another (i.e., showing off).

A home with *shalom bayis* proves that the ability to vigorously give of one's self to the other has been perfected. This is the open secret to any good marriage: to give, without expectation of getting anything in return, is to receive.[18]

Remember: the Aramaic root of the word *ahava*, "love," is *hav*, "giving."

> After his wedding, Freddie the groom bumps into his Uncle Yankie and says, "By the way, thank you for the wedding gift."
>
> "Oh, it was nothing."
>
> "That's what I thought, but my *kalla* said I had to thank you anyway!"

Here's what happens when *gematria* meets love and God:

The numerical equivalent of *ahava* (love) is thirteen. The numerical equivalent in the *yud-kay-vav-kay* name of God (which means "compassionate time-lessness") is twenty-six. When couples are in love according to the "ways of God"

---

16.   *Derech Eretz Zuta* 2.

17.   *Mishlei* 21:21.

18.   Remember: when it comes to giving, some people stop at nothing!

(which include *shalom bayis*), they merge the thirteen plus thirteen into twenty-six, defining the relationship of "loving friends" (*re'im ahuvim*) as one of Godliness.

The challenge for the spouse is not just to figure out what the other needs, but to provide it before the other person even realizes he or she needs it. Does this mean you must be a clairvoyant? No. You just need to talk openly and frankly in the home.

Failure to recognize the needs of others is a classic failure in communication; or as the Gemora puts it, "Unexpressed words are not words!"[19]

Hillel's "golden rule" ("What is hateful to you do not do to your fellow") doesn't apply in a marriage. Your spouse is not just a "fellow." The more appropriate Golden Rule of Marriage is to "treat your partner the way your partner wants and needs to be treated."

A close look at the structure of the Torah statement "When husband and wife merit to live in peace with each other, the Divine Presence resides in their midst,"[20] shows that it is also phrased in the *plural*, not singular conjugation.

Bringing the *Shechina* into your home is a collective effort!

> It's Monday morning and the *rav* is pleased with himself. "I must tell you," he says to his *shammas*, "I made nine people very, very happy over the weekend."
>
> "How so, Rabbi?"
>
> "I married off four couples!"
>
> "*Mazel tov*! But doesn't that only make eight people happy? How do you get the ninth?"
>
> "What! Do you think I do it for free?"

How can God tell if there's harmony in the household? When *both* husband and wife are equal in their desire to *give* rather than *receive*.

This is the opening, the window of opportunity for *shalom* to enter and stay, described by our Sages as no greater than "the space of the head of a pin." And since, writes the Zohar, "there is nothing that can stand in the way of one's will," this is wide enough that God promises in return to stretch the space "as broad as the opening of the *Ulam* [the entranceway to the Holy Temple]."

This *shalom bayis* rests on the foundation of three parties: we have already

---

19. *Kiddushin* 49b.
20. *Sota* 17a.

seen how the *yud* in *ish* and the *heh* in *isha* form God's name, implying the three-way bond in a marriage.

The moment the husband and wife become giving creatures, so does God, the third partner, Who then gives His protection and blessings.

Unless all three are involved, the efforts of any two combined to build an everlasting family edifice (*binyan adei ad*) will be futile. "Me" needs to become the royal "we," as in, not "What are *my* needs?" but "What are *our* (including God's) needs?"

> Sitting in the crowded coach section of the plane, Beryl is concerned that his pregnant wife is too crowded, so he asks an airline attendant, "Is there any way my wife can get bumped up to first class?"
>
> "Not unless we hit turbulence," she replies.

Shalom bayis withers on the vine unless there's a rich climate of giving.

After a *simcha* in New York, a young man offered Reb Yaakov Kamenetsky a ride home to Monsey. The man was surprised when Reb Yaakov, known for his extreme humility, asked if he could see the car first before accepting the ride. Reb Yaakov got into the back seat and sat for a moment. He then said he would accept the ride, explaining to the driver that he first had to make sure the seat would be comfortable for the *rebbetzin*.

One day Rabbi Aryeh Levine, the Tzadik of Jerusalem, took his wife to the doctor because her knee was in pain. The doctor asked what was wrong.

Rabbi Levine replied, "My wife's knee hurts us." He identified with her hurt as if it were his own.

Just in case your ego gets in the way of your generosity, the Midrash reminds us that everything God created depends on "giving" to another creation.

Thus, "the day borrows from the night and the night from day; the moon borrows from the stars and the stars from the moon; the sky borrows from the earth and the earth from the sky!"[21]

Through another Midrash, Shimon ben Eleazar adds, "Not a handful of rain descends from above without the earth sending up two handfuls of moisture to meet it."[22]

---

21.   *Shemos Rabba* 31:15.
22.   *Bereishis Rabba* 13:13.

In his famous *Nineteen Letters*, Rav Shimshon Raphael Hirsch elaborates: "Giving and receiving unites all creatures; none is by or for itself, but all things exist in continual reciprocal activity."

> A woman proudly tells her friend, "You know, I'm responsible for making my husband a millionaire."
>
> "Wow! What was he before he married you?"
>
> "A multi-millionaire!"

The key word here, in the context of marital harmony, is *reciprocal*.

If not reciprocated, giving is even worse than a one-way street; it's a dead end.

Philo, the first-century Jewish philosopher, put it bluntly: "Those who give, hoping to receive (even praise or honor), are in reality cutting a deal."

Not only is *shalom bayis* dependent on friendship, so is the Torah itself.

Torah is not an individual activity. Similarly, only friends and confidants, *together*, can jointly develop and pursue common interests and goals, akin to a spousal choreography which requires two to tango.

"Give me comradeship," Rabba quotes Choni Hame'agel (the circle-drawer), "or give me death!"[23]

"Two are better than one," is the advice from *Koheles*, "for should they fall, one can lift the other!"[24]

When asked to define the benefits of friendship, the chassidic master Reb Mordechai of Lechovitz replied, "Friendship is like a stone. A stone has no value, but when you rub two stones together properly, sparks of fire emerge!"

Shalom bayis is only sustainable through friendship. Make your spouse your closest confidant, a comrade-in-arms, a lifelong friend-partner. Remember: friendly partners do not pull in different directions; they combine their strengths to pull together for a common cause.

This is evident by the custom of close friends holding up the poles of the *chuppa*, a wedding canopy which symbolizes the couple's new home, supported in the future by friendship (making the *chuppa* from a *tallis* adds the symbol that the presence of Torah will cover ["protect"] the home).

---

23.   *Taanis* 23a.
24.   *Koheles* 4:9–10.

Without friendship, your marriage is akin to lyrics with no music; absent camaraderie your relationship is like a *chazan* without a voice.

> Yitzi and his wife sit down in the restaurant and the waiter comes over.
>
> "I'd like one hamburger and an extra drink cup," Yitzi orders. The waiter serves them and watches as Yitzi carefully divides the hamburger in half, then counts out the fries…one for him, one for his wife…until each has half. He then pours half of the soft drink into the extra cup and sets it in front of his wife. Yitzi begins to eat as his wife sits there watching, her hands folded in her lap.
>
> The curious waiter asks if he should bring another meal so they don't have to split everything.
>
> "Oh, no," Yitzi replies. "We've been married fifty years. We're the best of friends. We share everything!"
>
> The waiter then turns to the wife and asks, "Are you going to be eating something?"
>
> "Oh, of course," she replies, "but not just yet. It's his turn to use the teeth."

The Lubavitcher Rebbe on Spending Time with Your Wife

When the Lubavitcher Rebbe was recuperating from his heart attack in 5738, one of his doctors inquired into the Rebbe's daily schedule. Among the things the Rebbe told the doctor was that when he arrived home each day, he took time to sit with the *rebbetzin* over a cup of tea and converse.

"Upon your daily arrival home, I would recommend that you act in a similar manner," the Rebbe advised the hard-working doctor.

The *Shidduch* from Heaven

A person once asked the *Sfas Emes* whether to enter into a certain *shidduch* and he replied that this *shidduch* was *min hashamayim*. People close to the *Sfas Emes* were astonished when they heard that reply because the *Sfas Emes* rarely spoke in such a manner.

When he was asked about the incident the *Sfas Emes* explained, "Yesterday a man came to me and wept that he had grown daughters and no money. Everyone in town opposed him and he had only one friend in the entire town. How could he marry off his daughters?"

"Today," continued the *Sfas Emes*, "another man came and told me he'd been recommended that previous man's daughter for a *shidduch* and he'd inquired and been told good things about her. After a moment's consideration I realized that he must have inquired from that that 'one friend in the entire town.' If out of an entire town this man asked precisely this one friend, is this not a *shidduch min hashamayim*?"

The Pragmatic
Rabbi Zelig Braverman

Rabbi Zelig Braverman used to learn together with a man whose eyesight was severely impaired. The man once complained to Rav Zelig that his difficulty seeing was affecting his relationship with his wife because he was no longer able to perform many of his household duties. He asked Rav Zelig if he could help his *shalom bayis.*

A few days later, the man already felt and looked much better.

"You must have prayed very hard," he said to Rav Zelig, "because my wife is no longer full of complaints and our relationship has begun to improve considerably." Over the next few weeks, things worked out very nicely and *shalom* was restored.

But Rav Zelig hadn't prayed for him. Instead he did a little research and discovered that whenever the man went to *shul,* his wife would go out to do her errands. Rav Zelig took advantage of their absence and went to their house every morning to wash the dishes and tidy up. When the wife returned and found a clean kitchen she was extremely pleased to find that "her husband" was making a greater effort!

Rav Shlomo Zalman and His Wife Chaya Rivka

Rav Shlomo Zalman Auerbach married Chaya Rivka, daughter of Rav Chaim Leib Ruchamkin. When speaking at her funeral he made a stunning announcement: "Although it is customary to ask forgiveness from a *niftar*, I shall not do so. Throughout our entire marriage we never offended or hurt one another. We conducted our lives according to the *Shulchan Aruch*, and I have no reason to ask her forgiveness."

Rav Shlomo Zalman had a unique relationship with the *rebbetzin*. His son-in-law, Rav Yitzchak Yerucham Borodiansky, recalls one episode that shows the level of respect and honor that existed between them.

One day, Rav Shlomo Zalman's sister dropped in and, in the presence of the *rebbetzin*, asked her brother about a possible *shidduch* for her daughter. Rav Shlomo Zalman replied, "He's a fine boy."

When she left, Rav Shlomo Zalman quickly followed and caught up to her. Astonished at his behavior, she asked, "What's going on?"

"You asked me about a certain young man. But you should have asked your question in private."

"But who was in the room?"

"The *rebbetzin* was there, and why should she have to hear *loshen hora*?"

He then told her, "Don't go ahead with the match. He's not for your daughter."

Rabbi Acha on *Eishes Chayil*

Says Rabbi Acha: "Whoever marries a proper wife, it is accounted him as though he fulfilled the whole Torah from beginning to end. That is why it is all included in the *Eishes Chayil*, the last chapter of *Mishlei*, whose first verse begins with *aleph*, the first letter of the Hebrew alphabet, and whose last verse begins with *tav*, the last letter of the alphabet."

– Midrash

Rav Chiya on His Marriage

Rav Chiya's wife was known to cause him great anguish throughout their married life. Yet, whenever Rav Chiya saw an item that he thought she might appreciate, he purchased it for her as a gift. Rav Chiya's nephew, Rav, noticed this and asked his uncle why he went out of his way to treat her so graciously when all he received from her was abuse. Rav Chiya replied that "the fact that she raises our children and saves me from sin is sufficient cause for gratitude. The little aggravation she gives me is insignificant in comparison to the tremendous benefits she bestows upon me."

Rav Avrohom Pam on Words

"It is a pity that courtship – with its carefully honed phrases, so meticulously worded to avoid misunderstanding – comes to an abrupt end with marriage. Just as an unpleasant word can have devastating effects on a marriage, a kind word can do wonders to solidify a marriage."

– Rav Avrohom Pam, *zt"l, rosh yeshiva* Mesivta Torah Vodaas

"Honey, tomorrow's your birthday! What would you like most in life?" Tzvi asks his wife.

"Well," she says, thinking out loud, "I'd love to be ten again."

So the next morning, Tzvi gets up bright and early and takes his wife to a theme park. He puts her on every single ride in the park – the Death Slide, the Screaming Loop, the Wall of Fear. Five hours later she staggers out of the park, her head reeling and her stomach churning. Then Tzvi buys her popcorn, cola, sweets, a Slurpee and ice cream. Finally, the day over, she staggers home and collapses on the couch.

"Nu, dear," Tzvi asks proudly, "what was it like being ten again?"

His wife opens one eye and groans, "I meant dress size!"

Additional Free Tip(s)!

Be Attentive

> At breakfast, the wife tells her husband, "You know, last night I dreamt that you gave me a pearl necklace for our anniversary. What do you think it means?"
>
> "You'll know tonight," he replies.
>
> That evening, he comes home with a small package and gives it to his wife. Delighted, she opens it in excitement – to find a book entitled *The Meaning of Dreams*.

The best gift you can give your spouse is your time. So keep the courtship going. Chill out. Spend quality time *together*. Watch the sunrise or sunset *together*. Take days off. Get out more often.[1] Take short, quick vacations *together*. Take an ol' fashioned walk in the park. The activity is not as important as simply doing something *together*. Surround yourself with good, happy, friendly couples. Stay attractive and be attentive. Wives: cook your husband his favorite meals! Husbands: buy your wife flowers for Shabbas and a gift for *yom tov*! Feel good about yourself. Be creative and keep things interesting and alive. Call your wife during

---

1. Andy says to his wife Sarah, "Let's go out tonight, dear, and have some fun." Replies Sarah, "Great! But remember, if you get home before I do, leave the light on in the hall!"

the day, make her laugh, eat dinner *together* with your family every night,[2] and sing *zemiros* with your children at the *Shabbas tisch.*

Oh, one last thing in seeking marital nourishment: prayer helps.[3]

Zei matzliach and good luck!

> When asked how he had managed to make his marriage so successful, Freddie replied, "Well, it's important to stay close friends and go out a lot and get away from the house, the kids, the stress. Twice a week, my wife and I go to a nice restaurant and drink a little wine with some good food and interesting companionship. She goes Mondays, I go Thursdays!"

---

2.   I have a friend, a highly successful business magnate, who has been married for fifty-nine years. He told me his marriage works because he has never missed a "date" with his wife at home every evening for dinner at eight. He considered it a "sacred" meeting, and always said no to any other invitation he got that clashed with it.

3.   When the Torah describes Leah's eyes as "weak," our Sages tell us they were weak from crying because the Matriarch thought she had missed her destiny, marrying Yaakov. She prayed and her prayers were answered: she married Yaakov first. What's the most important aspect of prayer? A "fervent heart," a reminder of which appears, *twice*, in the *Sh'ma: b'chol levavchem,* "with all your heart." This does not come easy. In the olden days Jews would spend a full hour preparing themselves mentally and emotionally in order not to "clutter" their hearts with anything else before prayer. The more concentration, the better the chances! (*Brachos* 5:1, 5; *Rosh Hashana* 18a; *Sanhedrin* 106b; *Taanis* 2a)

Postscript

Lights and *Shalom Bayis*

Although time was first sanctified with Shabbas, space was not made holy until the arrival of the *Mikdash*. Both time and space are supported by light, the symbols of peace, and *both* husband and wife are allocated certain duties to reflect this.

The wife has the primacy of inaugurating Shabbas by lighting the Shabbas candles (*ner Shabbas*), whose flames increase the brightness of *shalom bayis* in the home. Shabbas is the day most associated with *shalom*; thus we greet fellow Jews with a "*Shabbat Shalom*" and we greet Shabbas by singing "*Shalom Aleichem*."

Meanwhile, it is the husband who inaugurates the menora of the *Mishkan* by lighting the Chanuka candles.

This explains why the laws of Chanuka are found in Tractate *Shabbas*: in order to reflect this common theme of *shalom* via lighting candles.

The traditional *bracha* that newlywed couples receive is to build a *bayis ne'eman b'Yisroel* that is filled with both *shalom* and *shleimus*, a home of "peace and wholesomeness."[1] This is why, if Shabbas candles are lit in a manner in which

---

1. Ironically, our rabbis tell us that the times before Shabbas and *yom tov* are especially tense times. In his sefer *Avodas HaKodesh*, Rabbi Chaim Yosef Dovid Azulai (*Chida*) claims these "busy" times are filled with a special *yetzer hora* (temptation) for husbands and wives to get into arguments. His advice? Couples should be extra careful and conscientious to be more respectful towards each other at these moments to preserve peace and calm (*Mishne Berura* 3).

their purpose (i.e., generating *shalom* in the home) is not fulfilled, you can't say the *bracha* over them.[2]

But there is a significant difference between the two lightings.

The Rambam, in his *Hilchos Chanuka* (Laws of Chanuka), stresses the dominance of Shabbas lights in the context of *shalom*: "If a person must choose between [purchasing] candles for Shabbas or candles for Chanuka, the Shabbas candles take precedence…because Shabbas lights symbolize *shalom bayis*."[3]

Additionally, if you only have enough money to buy Shabbas wine or candles, you buy the latter because of their link to peace in the home.[4]

"Household peace" is thus more important than illuminating the miracle of Chanuka.

Why?

Because Shabbas peace has proved to be an enduring family component of *shalom bayis*; in contrast, the peace in the House of the Maccabeans turned out to be temporary.

Less than two hundred years after the Hasmonean rededication of the Temple, the absence of *shalom* amongst Jews in the Holy Land led to the fall of the Second Jewish Commonwealth and the surrender of Jewish national sovereignty to Rome.[5]

And the Ramban adds an interesting insight: knowing that the menora, the world's oldest Jewish symbol, would continue to endure in the context of the *yom tov* of Chanuka, long after the Hasmonean dynasty faded into history, the Torah purposefully chose Aaron to perform the mitzva of lighting the menora in the *Mishkan*.

God wanted this important Jewish symbol to be permanently associated with the only Jewish leader known as an *ohev shalom v'rodef shalom*, one who "pursued and sought peace"!

2.   *Shulchan Aruch HaRav* 263:10.
3.   *Mishneh Torah, Hilchos Chanuka* 4:11–13, 14; *Shulchan Aruch, Orach Chaim* 678:1.
4.   *Shabbas* 23b; *Orach Chaim* 263:3; *Hilchos Chanuka* 4:14.
5.   *Shabbas* 21b.

Rav Nochumke of Horodna's Chanuka Lighting

It was a late Shabbas afternoon, following a gala *shalosh seudos* and an assembly of American *gedolim*, and Rav Yaakov Kamenetsky was speaking before the honored guests. When Shabbas was over and Rav Yaakov was still speaking, Rav Yaakov Ruderman left the room and returned a few minutes later. When the speech was over, Rabbi Ruderman apologized to Rabbi Kaminetzky for leaving in the middle of his speech and explained that he had gone to telephone his wife and let her know that he would be home late.

"I will tell you where I learned of the extent to which one must go to honor his wife," said Rav Ruderman to Rav Yaakov. "This is a story I heard from the holy *Chofetz Chaim,* who, in turn, heard it from his rebbe, Rav Nochumke of Horodna.[6]

"On one of the nights of Chanuka, Rav Nochumke sat beside his menora for a very long time before he lit the candles. The lights in all the other homes had been kindled much earlier, but Rav Nochumke's window was still dark. Finally, Rav Nochumke's wife entered the room and he promptly rose to light his menora. The students who were waiting with Rav Nochumke were confused by their rebbe's behavior since they were familiar with the opinion of the Ramban, who maintains that the mitzva to light the menora cannot be fulfilled after sunset. Therefore, they asked their rebbe this question: "Why did you wait for your wife and forfeit fulfilling the mitzva in accordance with the Rambam's opinion if, anyway, the *rebbetzin* is not obligated to be present for the lighting?"

Rav Nochumke explained with the Gemora in *meseches Shabbas*, which states that if a person must choose between lighting Chanuka candles and Shabbas candles, he should light Shabbas candles since the Shabbas candles are lit for *shalom bayis*. In other words, a mitzva which is performed to ensure peace in the home overrides the mitzva of Chanuka candles.

"Had I not waited for my wife, it would have hurt her feelings and, in that case I would have compromised my *shalom bayis* for the sake of Chanuka candles. If our Sages preferred that one light *Shabbas* candles over Chanuka candles in order to preserve *shalom bayis*, then I can certainly rely on the opinions of the other *meforshim* who allow for the candles to be lit after sunset."

---

6.   The *Chofetz Chaim* considered Rav Nochumke a symbol of kindness and kept his photo in his wallet to be inspired to emulate him.

PPS

The whole of the Torah is for the purpose of promoting peace.
— Gittin 59b, Mishlei 3:18, Yevamos 109a, b

Be of the disciples of Aaron,
loving peace and pursuing peace;
be one who loves others and draws them near to the Torah.
— Pirkei Avos 1:12

Rabban Shimon ben Gamliel said,
"On three things the world stands:
on justice, on truth, and on peace"
— Talmud, Derech Eretz Zuta

God's name is Peace.
— Shabbas 10b

The Talmud "signs off," in the last Mishna in Uktzin, with
"God found no better receptacle for blessing than the peace."
— Uktzin 3:12

PPPS

Woman to judge:
"That's my side of the story.
Now let me tell you his!"

****

Marriage is one of the few institutions
that allow a man to do as his wife pleases.

****

Behind every successful man
stands a surprised mother-in-law.

****

A good wife always forgives her husband
when she's wrong!

****

I love being married. It's so great to find that one special
person you want to annoy for the rest of your life!

****

The Torah says a man is incomplete until he's married…
And then he's really finished!

OTHER TITLES BY JOE BOBKER

Hardcover • 400 pp
ISBN 978-965-229-398-5
$14.95 • 70 NIS

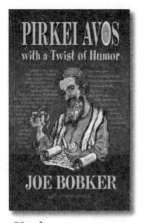

Hardcover • 312 pp
ISBN 978-965-229-419-7
$18.95 • 80 NIS

Hardcover • 422 pp
ISBN 978-193-014-396-8
$18.95 • 69 NIS

Paperback • 338 pp
ISBN 965-229-366-0
$14.95 • 70 NIS

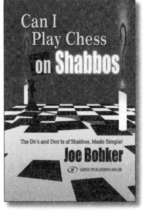

Hardcover • 308 pp
ISBN 978-965-229-422-7
$18.95 • 80 NIS

Hardcover • 280 pp
ISBN 978-965-229-378-7
$18.95 • 80 NIS

Hardcover • 336 pp
ISBN 978-965-229-448-7
$21.95 • 90 NIS

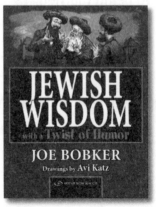

Hardcover • ~280 pp
ISBN 978-965-229-423-4
COMING SOON